OH CRAP!
I HAVE
A TODDLER

Also by Jamie Glowacki

Oh Crap! Potty Training

OH CRAP!
I HAVE
A TODDLER

Tackling These Crazy Awesome Years—
No Time-outs Needed

Jamie Glowacki

G

GALLERY BOOKS

New York London Toronto Sydney New Delhi

G

Gallery Books
An Imprint of Simon & Schuster, Inc.
1230 Avenue of the Americas
New York, NY 10020

First Gallery Books trade paperback edition June 2019

GALLERY BOOKS and colophon are registered trademarks of Simon & Schuster, Inc.

All names and many identifying details have been changed in the case histories discussed, and some individuals are composites.

For information about special discounts for bulk purchases, please contact Simon & Schuster Special Sales at 1-866-506-1949 or business@simonandschuster.com.

The Simon & Schuster Speakers Bureau can bring authors to your live event. For more information or to book an event, contact the Simon & Schuster Speakers Bureau at 1-866-248-3049 or visit our website at www.simonspeakers.com.

Manufactured in the United States of America

2   4   6   8   10   9   7   5   3   1

Library of Congress Cataloging-in-Publication Data

Names: Glowacki, Jamie, author.
Title: Oh crap! I have a toddler : tackling these crazy awesome years—
no time-outs needed / Jamie Glowacki.
Description: New York : Gallery, [2019]
Identifiers: LCCN 2018061341 | ISBN 9781982109738 (pbk.)
Subjects: LCSH: Toddlers. | Parenting. | Child rearing.
Classification: LCC HQ774.5 .G56 2019 | DDC 306.874—dc23
LC record available at https://lccn.loc.gov/2018061341

ISBN 978-1-9821-0973-8
ISBN 978-1-9821-0974-5 (ebook)

"What to Say Instead of Be Careful" by Josée Bergeron
used with permission of Josée of Backwoodsmama.com.

This book is dedicated to Pascal, the most
awesome kid a parent could ask for.
Seriously, he's the best.
He also ate a lifetime supply of cereal while
this book was being written.
And that's okay.

And to any parent trying to make their
parenting better.
I see you.
Thank you for allowing me into your lives
to support you.

CONTENTS

CONTENTS

INTRODUCTION

Toddlers, preschoolers, threenagers. Whatever we want to call this age, it is a tumultuous time. I like to call it psychotically awesome.

If you don't know me, I'm Jamie and the author of the wildly popular potty training guide *Oh Crap! Potty Training*. I've been a full-time potty trainer for over ten years. Which means that I work with this age group on the regular, with poop on top of personality. For real, literally.

Throughout my private practice, I've found parents to be confused about both mental and physical development in the three, four, and five years. And I've most definitely found that the sheer amount of information on the internet has muddled up parenting by a lot. I work with hundreds of families a year. Potty training doesn't exist in a vacuum. It exists right smack in the middle of toddler behavior. Over the years, I've seen parents get farther and farther away from appropriate developmental expectations for this age range. My potty training consults soon morphed into general parenting. I found myself communicating with more doctors, occupational therapists, psychologists, and parenting colleagues, as we all try to shift this strange pendulum swing.

This preschooler age range is wildly misunderstood. It's such a crazy time of growth and brain development. But the most important aspect of this age range is *individuation*. Individuation is the psychological process in which your child *individuates*, or separates from you to become an individual. Prior to these years, your child really believes that you and he are one and the same person. If he bonks his head, he thinks you feel the pain. Children this young are completely enmeshed in you because they have to be. They cannot survive without you.

Then begins this process of individuation, when they start to realize *Oh, hey! Look at this! I'm MY OWN PERSON.* And that brings the age of *no*. And all the attitude. And all the personality. And all the opinions. And ta-da! You got yourself a threenager. The term *threenager* has become popular vernacular for three going on thirteen, with all the attitude and seemingly psychotic mood shifts that are stereotypical of the hormonal teenage years. While some people feel this is a negative term, I like to think it's not: teenagers and toddlers are both awesome. Both experience explosive growth, coupled with a developmental need to push against and away from you, and in this way they're very similar. Just as for teenagers, toddlers' development *job* right now is to pull away from you. Not because they don't love and need you but because they have to find themselves. I don't mean that in a hippy-dippy way of "finding yourself." I mean they literally have to figure out who they are as a person, one who is separate from you. Which means a fair number of noes, the frequent can't-seem-to-choose, and, yes, the almighty power struggle.

But through it all, what we must remember is that this behavior is developmentally appropriate. Your child's own personality is emerging and there is something wildly wonderful about being part of this process. If, you know, you actually make it out alive, intact, and sane.

This blossoming personality makes this age *awesome*. But also slightly chaotic and more than just a little frustrating. To preschoolers the whole world is new. The whole idea that they are their own person is new. The fact that they have their own body and are starting to gain autonomy is new. So they seek control! Not only because it feels emotionally stabilizing, but because it's totally fun to control their own body, mind, and spirit. And hell, while they're at it, they may as well try to gain control of everything around them, including you!

This mission to gain control is not just about them being a pain in your butt. I mean, of course sometimes it's a straight-up pain in the butt. But mostly this is their learning process. This is how they'll grow into their own awesomeness.

One of my favorite parenting people/experts/philosophers/ whatever-you-want-to-call-them is Kim John Payne of Simplicity Parenting. He articulates something about parenting that I've known intuitively, and does it in a beautiful way:

> Zero to six years is governing.
> Six to twelve years is gardening.
> Twelve to eighteen years is guiding.

A few years back, I watched Payne give a talk at a local university. He was adamant that one of our main issues today is that too many parents have that order upside down. They are trying to guide in the zero to six years. I was all, *Aha! Yessss!* That's exactly what I find in my own practice and my own community!

See, the big problem is that toddler brains aren't ready to be guided. Their development is not ready for endless choices and good decision-making. They have low impulse control, low empathy, and almost zero long-term judgment. They need governing: rules and boundaries with real-life natural consequences. I find that's where a lot of parents get murky.

INTRODUCTION

Let me interrupt myself here for a minute, just so we're clear. I am, in fact, a big, fat, hippy-dippy parent; attachment parenting was my jam. I've always believed that children should be treated as the small humans they are. They should have choice and autonomy, and we shouldn't seek to control them. I don't believe in authoritarian, power-hungry parenting. I think children should be included in every aspect of our lives and not talked down to. I believe in honoring every child's developmental process, whatever that may look like. Every kid is a bud of fabulousness just waiting to blossom and share that with the world.

However, I also believe that we as parents have been on the planet a lot longer. We are the ones in control because we *know more*. We often (not always) know better than our new little beings who haven't been here all that long. Throughout this book, I will talk about power dynamics, about when we the parents should hold the power stick and when we can offer it up to the child. There is always a power dynamic at play. And if the child holds all that power, the whole house will be imbalanced.

But I'm getting ahead of myself here.

Let me prepare you for what I hope is the fun part. There are a shit ton of parenting books out there. I know. I'm in that world. And most of those books outline dos, don'ts, techniques, laundry lists, and ways to think about your behavior with your child. But what I see out in the world of parenting books is a gross misunderstanding of the challenges and development of the late toddler years.

We're expecting a thought process from toddlers that literally hasn't been formed yet, while skipping over some huge skills that the little kids are not only capable of but need to learn properly for the sake of their growth and development. Many parents are expecting reasoning, logic, empathy, and long-term judgment. And yet they completely underestimate their toddlers' ability for good risk assessment and life skills. Parents and kids are not on the same page. That's why I have written this book in two parts. Cleverly titled:

The Parent Part of the Book

and

The Kid Part of the Book

I will do my best not to simply spew ideas and theories at you, but will also give you practical tools, resources, and the examples of real-life situations that I've dealt with in my practice. All of parenting is one giant toolbox. The more tools you have, and the better you know how to use them, the more effective you can be. The development and growth of the preschool-age child is so lightning fast that you really need the right tools for the job. Often when I start working with a family, they aren't totally without skills or tools, but their tools no longer work. A common thing I hear is, "Well, we used to do x-y-z but it just doesn't seem to work anymore." Have you heard the saying, "Bigger kids, bigger problems"? As your child grows, the tools you have may be too simple for the complexity of her growing personality.

The later toddler years are like driving a Ferrari on winding mountain roads. You gotta be able to switch gears with barely any warning. You have 2.3 seconds to figure out which gear is best. The things that have worked in the past are no longer going to work. And this is great! It means your child is developing in personality, in brain, in spirit at a rapid rate. You gotta keep up.

INTRODUCTION

I remember my own parenting. I got cocky for a minute, which you *know* the universe hates and will smite you down for in a heartbeat. The minute you think you have something in the bag, you get thrown a curveball. Pascal was two. I was thinking, *Terrible twos? Whatever. I got this parenting thing nailed. I could do it on one foot, with my eyes closed.* Then he turned three. Literally the *day* my child turned three, the devil himself moved into my house. I was like *Holy shit!* None of my tools worked. I cried. A lot. And then I found more tools and a rhythm and a routine. I took a breath and thought of all my psychology training, all my social work, and I realized this was a dance. A magnificent dance with a new spirit finding his way.

I want to share that experience with you. Not just what I learned in theory and books, but what I've learned as a mom in the trenches—what I've learned in the ten years I've worked specifically with this age group. I know the modern pitfalls. I know what parenting today looks like and why it's so hard. I want to help you explore the joy and wonder that is the threenager. I want you to see their awesome and help it develop; let's manage the behavior so they can shine.

This book is a whole-body, whole-person approach to helping our toddlers and preschoolers be the best little people they can be. It's not a quick fix but rather an approach from the inside out. These years are about the blossoming of a personality, and that blossoming just naturally brings some difficult behaviors, to be sure. But there are also so many things we can do foundationally to bring out the very best in our kids.

I remember when my own son was little and I was talking to my mom one afternoon. In my personal life, I was having a hard time with another mom whose child was always in a mood, displaying wonky behavior. I liked the mom but she was always saying things like, "Oh. He's just tired. He's just hungry." And I would constantly think, *Well. He needs more sleep!* or *Okay. Feed him.* I started paying attention around me and realized how often I heard those two phrases, two seemingly simple things to fix. I was just dishing with my mom, saying, "What *is* that?"

And my mom said the most powerful words I've ever heard about parenting: "I don't know, Jamie. Some parents don't seem to want to give their kids the chance to be their very best. They don't set them up to be the best kid they can be."

Holy whoa, did that stick with me. It's greatly influenced my work with families, and it's the basis of this book.

There are natural challenges working against you and your child at this age. Individuation. Big emotions with limited language. A growing body that isn't always as skilled as your toddler would like. Emerging personality. These all contribute to making this age hard.

With all that going on for your little ones, my goal here is to help you to set them up for success: for good behavior and healthy minds, bodies, and hearts. To do everything in your power to help them be the best they can be. There will be lots that is out of your power; I'm not claiming to be a miracle worker. But let's work on everything that is within your power, yeah?

A few words about me before we begin. I mentioned my parenting style, so you already know how I feel about that. My writing style is irreverent. I cuss. I don't use proper grammar all the time. It's on purpose. I am vehemently against the "toddlers are assholes" premise in general—even though they can, in fact, be total assholes at times. I honor and respect the developmental process of all kids. Please don't mistake my irreverence for disrespect.

And listen. I work with kids. I am knowledgeable in this

area because it's my job. I work with families, I research, I collaborate with other professionals. I've learned a lot. I want to share what I've learned with you. *But you are the expert of your child.* Do not give me or any other expert power over that expertise. This book is meant to give you ideas, strategies, and springboards for understanding both yourself and your toddler's behavior. If something doesn't resonate, ditch it. I do not nor will I ever think I know more about your child than you. I see too many parents giving some expert all their power, going against their own intuition. I see too many parents who feel like a failure because something an expert said doesn't apply to or work with their child. Remember this: books are written for the general public. You must, *must* filter any ideas you find through what you know about your particular child and family dynamic.

You should also know that this book is written with the average, neurotypical child in mind. Though I run into many different situations and diagnoses in my work, I do not claim to be an expert on specific disorders or diagnoses. That said, there are strategies in this book that any parent can use regardless of whether her child has a disorder or diagnosis.

Think of this book as a collaboration, you and me working together. This isn't me on some high horse, telling you what to do. I am always humbled by working with parents and helping them to improve their skills and understand their child's development a little bit more.

You are a badass parent. Just know that.

THE PARENT PART
OF THE BOOK

Toddlers and preschoolers are lovably crazy. Don't get me wrong. You are going to see erratic behavior because their brains and physical bodies are exploding with growth. However, if that erratic behavior becomes the norm, that's when we as parents start drowning—and may blame it on the child. It's so easy to see a behavior in our kids and want to just fix that behavior in a vacuum.

We simply have to take some time to look at ourselves, and not just how we are as parents. We have to look at how we are as people. The reason this book is divided into "The Parent Part" and "The Kid Part" is that it takes two to tango. There are two parties involved here and neither is off the hook. If we look only at fixing kid behavior, we're not going deep enough for lasting change. Most parents come to me looking for a quick fix. "He's hitting everyone and it's uncontrollable." They want me to give them tools to stop the hitting, which I can do. But part of that tool-giving process is digging a little to find the root. The hitting is the symptom; we need to find the disease, if you will. The why.

Here's an interesting analogy for you. Fascia stretching versus muscle stretching. Fascia is the thick layer of tissue between your skin and the muscle. If you've ever gotten a really deep sports massage, those hands were busting through the fascia. The fascia holds the muscle in place. When most of us stretch or take yoga, we're stretching the muscle. It feels so incredibly good right after class. But then within hours, we're usually back to creaks and groaning. Because the fascia pulls the muscles right back into your habit. Say you sit at the computer all day for work, which many of us do. The fascia will start to curve in our upper backs. It will form to our daily, usually bad habits. You can stretch that muscle all day long, but that fascia is going to pull everything right back to the yucky ground zero.

I can give you all the tools in the world to help your preschooler, but you and your parenting are the fascia holding the situation in place. If we don't look at our own behavior and actions, it doesn't matter how many skills we can give our kids: if our behavior doesn't change, our kids' behavior will always snap back to bad habits.

I am not going to put more on your impossibly full plate.

However, it is literally impossible to fix a problem—any problem—without looking at what went wrong. Largely, when it comes to our toddlers, *we* are what went wrong. Let's take a minute, though, because I really don't want you to feel overwhelmed. We as parents are already blamed for a shit ton of things in society.

There is a whole lot of parent shaming going on in the world right now, gleefully documented on social media. Viral videos of imperfect parenting. Memes galore letting you know just how badly you're screwing up. All this is actually part of the problem. Everyone has an opinion about our parenting. But we'll dive into that can of worms in the following chapters.

When I say let's look at ourselves and dig deep, I'm not talking about trying to fix the two hours you let your kid watch the iPad so you could get a freaking break. I'm not talking about whether or not you feed your kid perfectly prepared organic meals.

I'm talking about soulful connection with our kids. I'm talking about examining ourselves to find *our* triggers, to find *our* unconscious contributions to toddler behavior.

So, let's start with you, the parent. Here's the deal: sometimes we get so mired in our kids' behavior we forget that *we* are the ones in charge. Which means *we* are contributing to the dynamic and thus the behavior. Yes. With the explosive brain development of this age, it's absolutely certain that some of your child's wonky behavior comes out of the blue. However, we have to look at ourselves.

How we are running the household, the rhythm and routine of each day.

How we are reacting, overreacting, or even underreacting.

How we feel as people, not just as parents but as spouses and in general. You matter. Your spouse matters. Your marriage matters. I see way too many parents completely sacrificing themselves at the altar of parenthood. Yes. Our children are demanding at this age. They physically need us for sure. But we *must* take care of ourselves.

Put on your own oxygen mask before assisting others.

Words to live by, especially in the first five years of your child's life.

This part of the book is about you and how you might become a better parent by working on yourself. You as a person who happens to be a parent. These may be ideas or concepts you already know and I'll just be reminding you, or these may be brand-new for you. Either way, take them to heart.

Unlike most parenting advice, this section goes beyond offering tools for interacting with your child. It also covers all the peripheral things you may not be aware of that affect how you interact with your child on a very soulful level. In other words, we all bring some shit to our parenting table that we think has nothing to do with the actual child or situation that is right in front of us, but surprise, it is part of the bigger picture.

None of this is theory. None of it is something I just came up with; I'm talking about the real issues real parents like you are struggling with. This is material I've garnered from all the families I've worked with. Deep parenting is hard work, but it's also extremely exciting. In the following chapters you may find some missing links that will help you better understand your struggles. My sincerest hope is that you have some big aha! moments that you can further explore with your partner. And with yourself, particularly if you're a single parent.

We'll be sifting through a few concepts:

- Boundaries! And why they are the crux of everything
- Why your parenting philosophy may be screwing you
- Connection, connection, connection above all else
- Parental martyrs and how to care for yourself
- How to literally get more time
- Parental anxiety, and the myriad things that exacerbate this anxiety
- Reactionary parenting: the good, the bad, the ugly

Let's jump in and look at ourselves first. How we can shore up our boundaries, find our own triggers, take care of not just our children but ourselves and our adult relationships.

And then we'll jump to "The Kid Part of the Book" and spend a bunch more time talking about those lovable rug rats and how to curb the crazy and turn challenging into charming.

CHAPTER 1

BOUNDARIES

We can't make a single move forward without talking about boundaries. Boundaries are truly the base of parenting. If you have any notion of good parenting or bad parenting, it's probably based in boundaries. In simple terms, these are the rules and expectations you have. We have personal boundaries that apply to our lives outside of parenting and we have boundaries with our kids. Having boundaries is one of the most confusing aspects for most parents because it may be at odds with your philosophy. I find many parents are doing what I call *oppositional parenting*.

This is when you were raised a certain way and it created some inner wounds for you. You then vow to *never* be that way with your own child. You go in the complete opposite direction from what your parents did. The problem here is that you may not be actively choosing your parenting skills. You may just be blindly doing the opposite of what your parents did.

Quick example: Let's say your parents made you sit at the table until every bite of food on your plate was gone, even if it was for hours. You swear that won't happen with your kids, so you don't make them eat anything they don't appear to like. In short order, you may end up with a crazy picky eater who never wants to sit at the table. Do you see? You didn't plan a mealtime routine. You just did the opposite and it got you into trouble.

I'm going to say this so many times you may want to puke,

but here goes: Kids are always learning. Always. It doesn't matter if we are actively teaching. They are always observing, picking up cues and nonverbal communication. *They are learning the rules of living in your family.* They are learning the rules of living, period. They are literally learning their place in the world. They are naturally going to fight to be alpha dog. They are naturally going push boundaries and then push some more. And they are super curious where the limits lie.

Here's the part that often gets lost in the shuffle of crappy behavior:

This is their developmental job.

It can look like total manipulation. It can look like a crazy pain in the butt. It can look like jerky, asshole behavior. It's not. Although, to be fair, sometimes it is. But again, learning how to *not* be an asshole requires being one, trying it on for size.

It's all learning.

We all do this. One day, you may be five minutes late for work. You look around and realize, huh . . . no one really seemed to notice that I was five minutes late. The next day you figure, let's see if they notice if I'm ten minutes late. You're going to push the limit. We all do. Until someone says, "*Stop it.* You can't do that." That might not be a good-enough warning for you, so you keep pushing. You may get fired. We all push the limits, find where they lie, push some more, and then deal with the consequences.

Your little one might try something on for size. Or maybe she's just feeling cranky. "No, Mommy can't sit next to me." You probably figure, Who cares? I don't have it in me to fight this right now. I can easily not sit next to her. Right?

And then it happens again and it seems so small and insignificant that you don't even blink. Until it becomes a thing. She won't let you sit near her all the time, then pretty soon she won't let you sit at the table. What starts to look like crazy, demanding behavior is her running with the power you gave her. That's "all."

This age range defines "If you give them an inch, they'll take a mile."

Since pushing boundaries is her job right now, your child can't be faulted for exploring her limits. The whole world is so new and exciting. She *has* to figure out her place in it. And that means testing the limits. Every limit. Every time. Everywhere.

It's then up to us to set the boundary. Boundaries are *the* key to life. Not just for us as parents but for us as people. I'm sure you've heard the word before, but let's get super clear because boundaries at this age are the foundation of the rest of your parenthood.

Boundaries are your lines in the sand that cannot be crossed without consequences. They are your rules, both personal and parental. They are your *no* and your *yes*. What you'll put up with, what you won't. Your "Oh hell no, you aren't doing that!" And we all have different ones, so you can't rely on someone else's boundaries. This is where a "parenting philosophy" can get sticky. If you are leaning too far into a particular philosophy without paying any mind to yourself and how you actually feel, you will be in deep emotional doodoo in no time. Feeling exhausted, depleted, and especially resentful means your boundaries probably need to be tightened up. Right now, it is important to remember that your child, particularly at this age and this stage of development, is going to push your boundaries as far as he can.

You are going to set a rule or a "no" in place, and here's what trips most parents up: the expectation that your little one will be cool with it. I'm telling you right now, it is his job to not be cool with it. It is his job to push against it.

15

I'll say that again (and again): It's a toddler's developmental job to push against your "no."

Which means your job is to hold firm.

This is the psychotic awesomeness of this age: once your child starts to push limits and realize she is her own person, with her own free will and choice, she will be mired in choice and control. So mired she can't decide. And if you choose for her, OMG, *it will be tragic.* If you've ever struggled with your child over what clothes to wear or what color cup to drink from, you know what I'm saying.

What ends up happening is that few of us have the time in a day to sit around holding boundaries. So we cave. We do whatever is necessary to get out of the house, out of the market, out of this crazy. And then your little one has learned something. What started as normal, developmentally appropriate high emotion has now become a learning tool.

How did my toddler learn this behavior?

When I'm working with a family, we simply have to explore: How did your child learn this behavior?

When a child is acting intolerably kooky, diagnoses notwithstanding, we *have* to look at how the child learned this behavior. Because he learned it somewhere.

Which usually means, we taught it. Unconsciously, yes. Unknowingly, certainly. Unwantedly, maybe.

We hear "limit testing" and "power struggle" so often, those words have almost lost meaning. Or somehow we think they are "bad" behaviors. But I want to reframe them as exciting. Seriously. What's more exciting than your child figuring out his place in your family, in the world? The bummer of course is that

16

it looks really crappy from where you're sitting, right? Because check out the trajectory of development:

Up until around thirty months, parenting has probably been a joy for you. Exhausting in a sleep-deprived way, to be sure. But mostly a joy. The astounding physical growth is so exciting. That first *real* smile at you at six to twelve weeks melts your heart. The learning to eat with fingers that can't even find their mouth. OMG. The camera is out in full force. Learning body control, starting to crawl, cruise, walk. Can this child do no wrong? And of course you don't have a huge bias or anything, but you're pretty sure you might have a genius. You get glimpses of the independence seeking, "I do," "Myself," but pretty much your child is still on the same page as you. Exploring, joyful, wanting to help. Caring about your opinion. The naked, unabashed love that flows between you is thick and gorgeous.

Then holy shit. Somewhere around thirty months, this crazy thing called individuation starts to happen. Children begin to realize they are different from you. Which means they can say no. Which means the quest for alpha dog status has begun. On your mark, get set, *limit testing*!

They start pushing those boundaries. What trips most people up, though, is that there's no actual Ready-Set-Go for this moment. They are little and sweet and this limit testing sneaks up on us. You may know that you'll have to set boundaries and consider "discipline," but not now! They're so little. Yes. They are. But their inherent quest for control will still be there.

I had this massive aha when I first started outlining this book. It had seemed obvious to me but I realized it is not obvious. What I'm talking about here is the difference between two years old and three years old. The specific transition between those specific years.

At two, they have not hit individuation. They care about

17

what you think, they care about pleasing you. Boundaries are fluid and don't have to be stringent. Then three hits and you think you still have the same sweet child who cares about what you think. But because of individuation, your little one doesn't give a rat's ass about what you think. So now those boundaries need to be strong! What gets tricky is that in many ways toddlers seem to be practically the same child at two and three, but psychologically, they are worlds apart.

Let me digress into an analogy, because "the quest for alpha dog status" is a real thing. Because of my history and my knowledge base, I've worked hard at my own parental boundaries. I'd say I'm pretty good at them, and in those zero to six years, I worked hard at maintaining boundaries. When Pascal was six, we got our first dog. Stella was a nine-year-old, seventy-pound, lab-boxer mix and came to us trained as far as house training and good in-home behavior.

But, oh my goodness, the minute I took her out of the house, this dog was psycho. She was highly reactive to other dogs, would yank my arm out to go sniff something (and I'm strong!), and God help me if a squirrel crossed our path. I sensed this wasn't normal behavior but it was fairly doable for me.

That is until we went on a vacation and my mom doggie-sat Stella. Out on a walk, Stella saw another dog and literally took my mother down and dragged her a bit, busting my mom's knee open. I started looking up doggie behavior online and found that Stella's behavior was "kill behavior": if she had to go to a shelter for some reason, she would be put down for this behavior. That is very bad behavior indeed and I'd had no idea; I had thought it was at least within normal range.

I immediately booked with a very fancy dog trainer. He followed us on a walk, watching our behavior. Then he sat me down to tell me some very hard truths.

18

I'll be repeating this fact several times through this book because I think it's such a good gauge. Your average dog and your average three-year-old are at the same level of brain development. Literally. Of course, dogs will stay there and our children will very quickly mature and develop more brain power. But it's a good marker when we try to reason with three-year-olds—meaning, of course, you can't. Reason hasn't entered the developmental picture yet.

Jeff the dog trainer pounded me with a severe reality check. He said everything about me was submissive to the dog. My body language said that I wasn't in control, I wasn't the adult human leading the show. My voice was pleading, not firm and confident. I sounded high-pitched and nervous. Most important, it seemed that I had the expectation that logic and reason would appeal to my dog.

Ouch.

He went on to tell me the things I knew but wasn't really getting. Dogs have little to no impulse control. Yes, they can be trained and taught, but on their own accord? Nope. Dogs will groove with an alpha dog. They will fall in line and follow the alpha. And here's the really important part: If there is no alpha, the dog will try to be the alpha. If there is no one telling the dog what to do, the dog thinks that it is her job to lead and protect and be the alpha. I say "think," but it's really more of a primal action.

The nuts and bolts looked like this: I was to walk in front of her at all times, leading her and keeping her body behind my body. I was to keep the leash very short and not let her randomly jolt off to sniff something. I was surprised and said, "But this is her walk, doesn't she get to sniff?" Jeff said, "No. It's not her walk. She must do what you want her to do; otherwise her behavior will get out of control. The joy for a dog is that she is not out in the wild. She gets fed and kept warm and safe. She gets your love. She doesn't get to do whatever she wants. If she starts to do whatever she wants, she will think she's the alpha and that *you* are under her control and protection."

It is up to me to be the alpha. I physically and mentally have to be in charge. All my nonverbal communication, everything about how I move and act, has to say, "I got this. I have you under my wing. You don't need to control anything right now."

Oooooh. As he's talking, I'm thinking, *This is so similar to parenting. This is so similar to how I work with both my parenting and potty training clients.* How'd I miss this with the damn dog? Well. Because she's cute. And I didn't know. And she seems almost human, so I forgot that although her capabilities might be stunning for a dog, she's still got limited brain development.

Lest Jeff sound like a hard-ass, he also was shockingly deep about raising a dog. Dogs live and die by our nonverbal communication. He said, "Anytime you leave the house, think, 'My dog is awesome. I love this dog so much. I am in control. I am the boss and my dog is awesome.'" He pointed out that once a dog's behavior escalated, everything in our nonverbal communication said, *I have a crappy dog. This walk is going to be awful. She's going to be bad.* And it's true. She had become so unmanageable outside the house that I was afraid of the dog. I was fearful of the small being in my charge.

OMG. Right? The similarities to three-year-old behavior blew me away. I was floored that I had missed this, but I kept spinning this round and round in my head concerning my work with families.

If we don't "govern" in those zero to six years, the child will simply, in a primal instinct way, say, *Okay. If you aren't going to be the alpha, I will.*

Toddlers will always seek control. If we really sit back and think of them as new blank slates, we'll have a better understanding of this. They are indeed very new. They've been on the planet for two or three years. Everything is new and exciting. Everything is an exploration. I often say behavior that looks "bad" is often curious behavior. Figuring out the world around them demands manipulation, demands mistakes, demands seeking control. It invites a literal, *Who's in control here?*

The problem is they don't yet have the brain power to handle that job. They don't have a large amount of impulse control. They don't have the extended thought process or long-term judgment to handle this job. Like a dog, they'll run right out of your front door and into traffic because *Squirrel!!!*

What are the different kinds of boundaries?

We simply must be the ones in charge. I often compare boundaries to a fence: a mental, emotional fence. We put fences up in our yard, yes—to keep things out but also to keep our children in. We don't let toddlers out the front door and expect them to make well-informed, sound decisions. Same with parking lots, right? We don't get toddlers out of the car and leave them to cautiously cross the parking lot, being mindful of cars, taking the quickest route to the store, totally on their own.

We just don't. This is an important parallel to how we work with the natural grain of toddler development, so let's take a minute to really break this down.

In a parking lot situation, we know the child is little, we know the child is not yet aware of exiting cars, watching for taillights in reverse. We know he'll run around, not watching for the adult things we know to be cautious of. We know that he is physically smaller than most rearview mirrors can see. We know he is so spontaneous in his body that the minute we release him from the car seat, he will become a little Tigger, bouncing all over the place. We know that the child might be super stoked about the treat you promised him if he can be good in Target, so we know he might bolt for the store. Or get sidetracked by that really cool motorcycle in the lot. Or think a quick game of hide-and-seek behind those cars would be really fun.

Basically, because parking lots have the potential to be death traps, we completely and pretty unconsciously tune into to our kid's lack of impulse control. We know and understand this and we're on high alert to be in complete control. Very few parents fuck around in parking lots. *Hold my hand. Right now.*

We speak firmly, unflinchingly. There is no room for negotiation. There is no pleading in our voices. We don't have an opinion or a parenting philosophy around it. We simply know that our little ones are not yet very capable of impulse control here. This is where, like Stella and me, we keep them on a short leash and lead the way. Being commanding and firm but also loving and kind.

And why does this happen so naturally in a situation like a parking lot?

Because we have to keep our children safe. Plain and simple. Physical boundaries tend to be easy because the danger is so obvious. In the parking lot there is a right way and a wrong way to behave. You as the grown-up know the right way, and you impose strong boundaries. This isn't a place to experiment. The margin of error is simply too narrow to mess around with.

Emotional boundaries tend to be trickier, but *the essence is the same.* Parenting at its core is about keeping our children safe and alive and thriving. Boundaries keep the child safe, both physically and psychologically. As in the parking lot example, we tend to be really on with our physical boundaries. They are easy to see in actual real life. (In fact, as we'll discover later on, most of us have *too* stringent physical boundaries when it comes to our children.) It's the mental and emotional boundaries that confuse most parents. Mental, emotional, and psychological boundaries are harder to define, harder to understand. Boundaries can be a tricky concept if you haven't really worked on them. I tend to run in Brené Brown-ish circles and I'm pretty sure I've paid for at least one house for my therapist with all the work I've done on my own boundaries. I work *hard* at boundaries. Most of us have to. It's easy to let them get loosey-goosey otherwise.

A real-life example—bedtime

When Liz and Dave first contacted me, Liz was practically in tears. Their little girl Riley had amazing behavior for Dave. He would say something once and Riley would hop to it. Like most parents, they both worked full time so they often switched child-chores between them. When Liz did bedtime or dinner, Riley would *draaaaaag* everything out. She would demand more at bedtime, so much more that she was extending her bedtime by almost an hour and a half. She'd demand more stories, more songs, more potty time, more night snacks. Though her daughter was in a crib, Liz would have to wait until Riley said it was time for bed, literally letting Mom know when she was ready. Any attempt to put Riley in the crib too soon would result in a massive tantrum. And, yeah, tantrums at bedtimes are a special version of hell.

Later in this book, we'll cover sleep and kids. But you should know right now that if my work was a pyramid, sleep would be the wide base. Sleep is *everything*; I treat it as an actual nutrient, and no matter what behavioral issues parents need coaching with, we always look at sleep first. An underslept toddler (a rampant occurrence these days) doesn't stand a chance at being her best self.

So naturally, the big red flag with little Riley is the fact that her bedtime is now being delayed by an hour and a half, sometimes even two hours. You know how there are dog years? A two-hour delay in a toddler's bedtime is like nine hours in toddler-sleep years.

Not only was that delay messing with Riley's circadian rhythms and making it seemingly impossible for her to actually fall asleep, it was also making her sleep later in the morning. Liz would have to wake her from a sound sleep, and hell hath no fury like a toddler woken from a sound sleep. Breakfast was rushed to get her out of the house on time. The whole morning routine was just cramped and yucky for everyone.

All kids, but especially kids in the toddler/preschool age range, need slow transitions. They just don't react quickly: they need to move slowly from thing to thing. This morning routine was agitating Riley, aggravating Liz and Dave, and setting up a disaster of a day.

We worked backward, as I'm prone to do. Why are mornings a mess? Because Riley is sleeping so late. Why is she sleeping so late? Because bedtime is getting too late. Why is bedtime getting too late? Because Riley is running the bedtime show, being demanding and holding her parents hostage with a potential late-night tantrum.

Toddlers are often jokingly called tiny dictators by their parents. I have literally heard the terms *dictator*, *tyrant*, *terrorist*, and *holding hostage* in conjunction with toddlers. Those are some pretty strong words for a little one who probably weighs in the thirty-pound range, does not in fact command an army, and has no complicated war strategy.

As I've already said many times, it's developmentally appropriate for little kids to be this demanding. But it's not okay to give in to those demands. As I've both heard and said thousands of times: We do not negotiate with terrorists. They can't handle the power.

If you've been around any kid for any length of time, you'll know that for a child to admit being tired is akin to a pacifist committing mass murder. "*Noooooo* . . . I'm *not* tired!" In the face of this dug-in resistance, Liz and I had to find not only ways to shave massive time off the bedtime routine but also ways that Liz could step into her strength as a parent and be the one in charge.

How do I start setting boundaries?

Setting boundaries can feel mean if you're not used to setting them. The problem is, if your boundaries are weak, you end up getting stepped on. And *then* you end up feeling resentful and exhausted. Let me give a few examples outside of parenting to better explain. Sometimes it's hard to see boundaries within parenting because our kids are just so precious to us.

I often use this example with clients because it's so clear and also personal.

My parents and I share a two-family home, and when my sister visits from Oregon, she and her family technically stay with them. I say technically because she's got two boys, sandwiching Pascal's age, so really, the whole house becomes a crazy zone of Nerf bullets, hide-and-seek, and boy central—loud, chasing, video gaming.

Pascal is a solo kid, and although he can hang with the best of them, we are pretty low-key when we're home. He often burns out in these situations with other kids. He's not accustomed to the very normal sibling bickering. He's just not accustomed to having people around all the time. So before these visits, we discuss how he can be his own advocate for taking breaks when needed.

One evening, my younger nephew was at our house and Pascal was just being awful. My nephew couldn't say anything right. Pascal would jump on him and correct the littlest thing.

I mean to a ridiculous level. He could say, "The trees are green." And Pascal was all, "Actually, the leaves are kelly green and there *is* brown bark." I mean that kind of ridiculous. I could see each little snide comment hurting my nephew's feelings.

I pulled Pascal aside and I said, "Hey, what is going on here?"

He said, "Mom, I really need a break."

"Just tell him you need a break. He can go down to Mem's house, no problem."

"But that would be so rude, asking him to leave."

"You are being ridiculously rude to him now. You are being so snippy, I can see you're hurting his feelings."

I intervened and told my nephew that we needed some quiet time. Not a problem; he went bouncing down to my parents' house without any big deal at all. And Pascal and I had a long talk about it. I use this example a ton with families I work with because it's such a classic example of when boundaries go bad.

Pascal was convinced that asking his cousin to leave would be rude. And yet he got himself so tired and resentful that he was actually hurting his cousin's feelings by being—you guessed it—rude. And in reality, the kid had zero problem giving Pascal a break. None. We too often assume that when we lay a boundary down, say no, are clear about our needs that the other person will think we are mean or rude.

This is super important and the big takeaway: People love knowing our personal rules. When the people in our lives have clear boundaries, we know and understand what to expect from them. When a person tells us no, we can't do something, most times we are like, "Okay! Great! Thanks for letting me know!"

Compare that to a person with weak boundaries, who will hem and haw, not give a straight answer, or do something for us but with bitterness and resentment. *That* is far more unpleasant than if that person had just said no.

It doesn't matter who you are or who you are dealing with; it could be extended family members, your children, your spouse. If you have weak boundaries, you will eventually feel exhausted and resentful.

Do you find yourself saying yes to things you really don't want to do? Or don't really have the time to do? And please don't get me wrong; there are times when we all have to suck it up to do something we don't want to. But I'm talking about on a regular basis. Boundaries—for all people, not just parents—are super important for keeping our mental and physical energy clean and intact.

If boundaries are important to everyone, I'm willing to say that boundaries are paramount to good parenting. Setting and keeping them is about the most important aspect of parenting. Because good boundaries in parenting make our children feel safe.

I've spent a good amount of time talking about why our little ones can't handle being in charge. I've talked about how being the alpha dog in the family isn't developmentally appropriate for kids. But now I want to talk about actual psychological safety. If we look at boundaries like a mental or emotional fence, just like a physical fence, they keep our children safely within those parameters. If we keep moving the fence, the child is on constantly shifting mental ground.

If one day a certain behavior gets a soft talking-to, and the next day the same behavior makes Mom lose it, that is very psychologically unsafe for the child. You as a parent become an unpredictable powder keg.

How do I communicate boundaries?

Marley and Jim consulted with me because Marley felt all over the map with her parenting. She had three kids very close in age, and most times, her house felt like chaos that she just couldn't rein in. She was mostly heartbroken because she felt she couldn't be the parent she wanted to be. She felt like every three or four days, she'd completely lose her shit and become a screaming banshee. She was starting to see fear in her children's eyes and was at a loss as to how to fix it.

Marley had grown up in an emotionally abusive home. She was committed to being a soulful parent, honoring her children's feelings, really listening to them, and not being passive-aggressive. She balked at the word *discipline*; for her, discipline was an authoritarian practice and its users power-hungry. She would talk gently to her children, spending a great deal of time explaining why and how their behavior was disruptive and not really acceptable. She would use those actual words, "not really acceptable." Think for a minute about that phrase and how wishy-washy that can sound to a child whose brain development is at the black-and-white stage, the good or bad. That's too much gray area for a toddler.

She was also talking too much. In later chapters, I will dive into all the reasons we need to shave down our talking, but in this particular situation, it simply wasn't effective. I don't care how anyone parents, really. My question to families I work with is this: Are you being effective? Because if you're not, find another way.

Marley's words and reason and logic were not effective with her kids. In one common scenario in their house, the kids would literally get into food fights at breakfast—throwing food all over each other and the kitchen. Marley would try to gently intervene, but in reality she had to wait till the kids were done throwing food. She'd clean the mess, explain to each child why this was not really acceptable and how she knew they could have better behavior tomorrow.

The only problem? Same thing the next day. And she'd do the same thing. Einstein's definition of insanity is doing the same thing over and over expecting different results. So Marley had a problem: she was not being effective. But the bigger problem arrived every every fourth or fifth day, when she'd *lose it*. And I mean epically. Screaming, out-of-control, mom-gone-crazy mode. To the point of scaring the kids.

Here's the deal: we all lose it at some point. Children can be frustrating and maddening. The question then becomes, How can we keep the losing it from building up inside us till we explode?

Marley had admirable parenting goals, particularly considering her own upbringing. But by not having strong daily boundaries (which felt mean and authoritarian to her), she was actually creating the very thing she was trying to avoid. Her children started to feel unsafe with her. If one day throwing milk across the kitchen gets a soft talking-to and then next day it creates a crazy mom, your child will be on unstable emotional ground. Do you see that?

I love where the general parenting pendulum has swung. We've learned so much more about child development. While conscious and unconscious abusive parenting still exists, there has been a huge shift. We are trying to really honor our children as little humans. We try to really listen and give weight to our kids' feelings. We don't just shove them off. But the pendulum has swung too far. Boundaries sometimes shift into no-man's-land.

Our kids are going to push until they find our boundaries, good or bad, strong or weak. That is a well-known psychological fact. If kids don't get a no, if we don't put up that emotional/mental fence, they will keep pushing forward until they find it.

That's where we get those horrible teen boot camp segments on shows like *Dr. Phil*. A kid will keep pushing and pushing and pushing until he is met with a parental boundary. And as his behavior escalates, the parents get more and more fearful of the child's reactionary behavior and more fearful of setting that firm boundary.

Why would a child keep pushing that boundary? *To feel safe*.

Much like swaddling for a baby, loving constraints feel safe. If you think of why we swaddle a baby, it's because they flail their limbs. They don't have much motor control, right? And that flailing of limbs gets their nervous system all jacked up, which makes them cry and fuss because, OMG, *Mom and Dad help me feel safe!* Almost every child instantly responds to swaddling. It soothes their nervous system and calms them.

Boundaries are emotional swaddling as your child grows.

Every family I have ever worked with has had some issue

with boundaries. Creating firm daily boundaries feels hard to most parents, largely because a parenting philosophy has run amok, because parents are exhausted, or because most parents don't realize how much of a foundation they are laying right now. What can seem like "Eh, this is just a difficult stage" can blow up into dangerous behavior later on.

With Marley and her family, we worked really hard on her daily boundaries of *no, you do not do that*. We worked on more governing at this age, since the guiding was ineffective (as it will be). We worked on her mental state: that being firm and grounded did not mean she was being mean or not listening to her children. And even if it *felt* that way, consistency in her behavior was 100 percent better than the two ends of the crazy spectrum that was actually scaring her kids. Super nice mommy and psycho mommy were not creating the emotional safety that was at the base of her parenting goals.

Power dynamics

We've talked about the psychological safety of reining our kids in with our family rules and expectations. There's another sliver here about boundaries that can make parents wiggly. And that is *power*. Power and parenting can give some people a peculiar feeling, like they shouldn't hold power over their children. "Power struggles" might be one of the most googled toddler terms. It has a rather nasty connotation.

I don't believe in holding power over our children. I don't believe in arbitrarily holding or withholding things over them. It is worth noting, however, that there is always a power dynamic happening. I think of it as a stick, or a wand if you're Harry Potter–inclined (as I am). It's not good or bad in and of itself. It's the intention with which it's used that matters. We certainly hand over that power wand to our children at various times throughout daily life. I find this is a good visual when you might feel murky about pushing back when boundaries are being overstepped.

As the grown-ups in our children's lives, we really should have the power wand most of the time. Not because we're power-hungry, but because we know things. We know better than our little ones because we've been on the planet a whole lot longer than them. We have long-term judgment and critical thinking. We have made a shit ton of mistakes and know for a fact that if you put your hand in fire, it will get burned. Our little ones don't know this yet. And while I'm a huge proponent of kid risk-taking, they just aren't capable *yet* of making good decisions.

They aren't yet capable of understanding the full magnitude of some of the risks they are taking.

So we hand over the power wand when we can, when it's appropriate, for things like choosing the bedtime story. Or between the red cup and the blue cup. If the child gets to hang on to the power wand, things start to get wonky. They get power drunk and start directing your actions willy-nilly. They start making unreasonable demands, particularly with us and our action, proclaiming where and when we can sit or what rooms we can enter, or crying because we started the car. They aren't developmentally ready to hold the power wand all the time.

Given too much power, your child won't actually feel safe. She will push and push for that safety. What's so confusing is that that push often looks like bad behavior. If the child could clearly articulate this, it would be something along the lines of "I don't feel comfortable here so I'm going to act out until you tell me where I can stop." Often, escalating behavior that pushes boundaries is your child asking for a limit. "How far can I go? *Please tell me.*" The kid, of course, doesn't have the words or the awareness to say this yet, so she speaks with her actions.

What's gotten so skewed is our philosophy. We think being firm is limiting the spirit of the child, when really, having limits allows your little one to feel safe and let that spirit blossom. Your child's psyche can't grow if he is constantly working out where his limits are. I'll go back to the fence analogy. We literally fence in our yards and parks, right? Because we know our kids don't understand the world and all the dangers that lie outside that fence. We know that if we didn't fence them in, they would run out in the street without looking. They would wander and get lost.

Now, some kids are going to try like hell to get out of that fence, especially if they aren't used to having a fence. They might try everything to get out of the fence, frustrated that they can't. But then something miraculous happens (and I have seen this literally play out in various playgrounds). Once the child realizes her limits, she learns to explore within that fence. She finds other kids; she starts using the slide, the swings, the sandbox. There's a whole small world to explore within the fence—an age-appropriate world—with other kids the same age.

For parents looking on, it can be tempting to think that the child really wants to explore the world outside the fence. *In reality the child is testing her limits.* If she was to get outside the fence, you'd be chasing her down as she flails. She's too little for the big-world rules, for crossing the street, for approaching dogs on the sidewalk. She will throw herself into situations that she doesn't understand, and that's dangerous. If you're constantly monitoring for danger, you can't really be developing spirit.

We've all seen or experienced the child who escapes a parent's grasp in a parking lot. That child is like a pinball in a machine. He has no concept of which way to go or what to do. In fact, he probably looks a little maniacal. You've seen that, right?

Now, think of that fence analogy in the child's mind and inner world. If the child is constantly having to test where your limits lie, he actually isn't doing the developmental work he needs to be doing. He is so busy figuring out where *you* are, figuring out his limits, that he isn't actually playing and learning and developing his inner life. It's a constant power struggle, even if just an inner one.

When we have clear rules and boundaries, when we can say no with our parental authority and the child knows we mean it, that child can do a child's job, which is to play and discover.

When to cave and when not to cave

Let's take a look at a super common boundary scenario that almost all of my clients deal with in some version or another. It comes in many different colors, so for an across-the-board title, I'll call it When You Say No but Eventually Give In. And we are, all of us, guilty of this. Here's an example I'm pretty sure we're all familiar with:

You're at the market, you've waited in line for twenty minutes with a full basket of a week's worth of groceries. Your little one sees candy in the checkout line (thank you, marketing people) and asks you for some. Okay, let's be honest, it's not exactly asking. More like whines and starts to whimper for the candy. You say no. The whining starts to escalate. But still you say no. And you can tell your child is starting to ramp up and you know where this leads. The store's busy. People are looking at you. You still say no but can feel your reserve starting to crack. You know you could take your child out of the store, but *really???* You're exhausted. You need these groceries. You've already waited in line for twenty minutes. You know the "right" parenting thing is to not give in, and if the child throws a fit, you are supposed to buck up and deal with the nasty onlookers. Or take that child and leave.

You know this is what you're "supposed" to do. But you cave. You say yes. Because it's easier and you need this fucking break right now. I totally get it. I've been there and I completely understand the cave-in. Of course, the problem then becomes that your child has just learned that escalating her behavior will get her the thing she wants. That's just a fact. If you take all the emotion out of it, she's simply learned that if you say no, she can bug you and ramp things up till you say yes. We'll talk more about this in the tantrum chapter. For now, I want to give you an actual real-life tool in these scenarios.

Because there's another dynamic happening here that's even more crucial than her learning a behavior. And that is the power dynamic. If your child can demand something and manipulate her behavior to get it, she has the power wand. She's running the show, so to speak. In this kind of situation and any situation remotely resembling this one, you must have the power wand. Otherwise, your child will run and run far with that power.

What I have parents practice and cultivate is this: split-second decision-making. When you find yourself in one of these situations, do a quick calculation: am I going to give in anyway? You know yourself, your level of patience at any given moment, and you know your child. If you even suspect you will cave, then give it right away. That's right. Give the candy or whatever right away. I know that probably goes against all other parenting advice you've ever come across, but hear me out.

Giving in right away puts the power wand back in your hands. It also makes you generous. And, yes, it avoids the escalation. But your parental power isn't weakened and it's far better to do a hard, fast yes than a yes after your child has manipulated the situation. Of course, with toddlers you run the risk that once means always, but you can set ground rules around that. Before going into a store you can tell your child, "Last time, we got some candy at the checkout. We do that sometimes. Today we will not, so please don't ask." Preparing the child in this way is far more likely to have a good end result.

Now, it may go without saying, but I'll say it anyway: you probably don't want to get your child that candy, period. I'm not saying give your child whatever he wants. It's important to notice the distinction between giving him a fast yes (because you know you don't have it in you to stay firm in a no) and just saying yes to everything. Maintaining boundaries you set is paramount, except, of course, when real-world exhaustion and low patience leave us primed to teach a very different lesson.

A no should be a no that no amount of crying or fit throwing will make you cave on.

A yes is yes.

There can always be a yes, as long as you are in control of the situation. Because if you're not, then your child is.

I think one of the trickiest things about boundaries is that life is a constantly moving target. So there's some quick thinking to be done. If you can master this split-second decision-making process, I can guarantee that it will change your parenting life. Because here's the thing: we have to factor you and your soft spots too. We have to factor in your vulnerabilities. You can't be a hard-ass all the time. And even if you could, would you want to? That's not fun. Parenting is hard and there are rules. For God's sake, you're helping shape a whole human being. Sometimes it takes my breath away, the work we're doing is so astounding and profound. But it's also *your* journey as well. It's not just childhood, it's parenthood too. You get to have your down days.

Before we delve into some parental self-care, let's dig a little bit more into parenting philosophies and why they may be screwing you.

The Big Takeaway

Boundaries are knowing when to say yes and when to say no. It's clearly communicating your limits, your capabilities, and when you've had enough. If you're not used to setting clear limits, this can feel mean. The reality is, everyone in your life will be better off knowing your boundaries. Children at this age need to know your limits and boundaries; otherwise they'll free-fall through their little lives.

CHAPTER 2

PARENTING PHILOSOPHIES

In the last chapter, I mentioned a few times that parenting philosophies—our idea in our heads about how we will parent—can get in our way. This problem bears some exploring since it's so prevalent in the parenting culture.

Whenever I work with a family, inevitably the words "parenting philosophy" come into play.

So many couples get pregnant and dive down the rabbit hole of getting a "parenting philosophy." Which is a lot like a birth plan. It's an awesome thing to think about. A few generations ago, no one thought of this stuff. You went in to have your baby and did what the doctor told you. Afterward, you followed up with the doctor and did what he told you. Yeah. Chances are the doctor was a he.

Most parents in my mom's era didn't think one bit about birth plans or child rearing. Then we, their children, all ended up in therapy and realized . . . hmm, maybe there's a better way to parent. The birth of the internet gave us a billion theories and opinions, some good and some bad. And so we started wading through them. And crafting a plan. Raising another human is one of the most important jobs on the planet and we have done our due diligence. We're not leaving anything to chance. We're going to make a plan for this child and how we will raise her.

That is fantastic. Except, as with a birth plan—or really any plan—things don't always go according to it. Like, the actual kid you have. That child may need a different style of parenting. A common complaint I hear is "I can't seem to be the parent I want to be." As we all prepared to be parents, we envisioned gentle scenes filled with love. We wouldn't ever yell or think of swatting a little behind. Bedtimes would be quiet and easy. Mealtimes a joyous celebration of home and hearth. Um. Yeah. No. We all know how *that* particular plan pans out.

One of the dangers of being entrenched in a philosophy or a big idea is that you can miss the actual child in front of you. The big idea looms above but it's not necessarily how it's going to actually play out. The problem, of course, gets compounded because often there's nothing *dire* on the line. For example, if your birth plan goes awry, you may have to mourn that later, but in the moment, you're going to go along with interventions because the safety of mom and child are on the line. It's an immediate decision. When a philosophy goes awry, it's never that dire a situation. It's small, little dings that chip away at the family dynamic; you don't notice it's falling apart until it's a mess.

Largely, I would say that most parents believe in *attachment parenting*, a philosophy I definitely agree with. But attachment parenting has led to a broad spectrum of dynamics that can get wonky. The idea behind the philosophy, of course, is that your child should feel securely attached to you. That doesn't necessarily mean physically, actually attached to you, although cosleeping and baby wearing can be components. A secure attachment, as widely recognized, means that the child feels secure and protected by her primary caregivers. She can depend on them for stable reactions; she can rely on them to help soothe her; she can depend on them to return when they have left. We also use the term *bonded*. Children who are securely attached generally are more self-reliant and independent as they grow, and they display higher self-esteem as well as better social relationships. Well. Okay, then! Sign me up! I want that for my kid. Who wouldn't?

One example I see quite often of attachment parenting gone sideways is with cosleeping. Mom and child may cosleep and Dad either gets no room or is left to a spare bed or the couch. In some families that may be perfectly okay, as long as everyone is getting the rest they need. However (and I will constantly say this): is it working for everyone? Is Dad really happy about being on the couch? Or are you really okay with restless sleep due to little feet kicking your face?

If it's not working for everyone, then something has to change. Philosophy has to be put aside. Parents will argue the philosophy and how good it is for the child and that it's a sacrifice and we all have to make sacrifices for our kids. However, if it's not working for the family as a whole, then it's not working. Resentments and hurts will start to build that will only add another kind of dynamic to the family. A not-good one.

When life revolves around your toddler

Another big problem with holding too firm to a philosophy is that, like in the cosleeping example, the pendulum can start to swing too wildly to one side, where it's all about the child and the rest of you get thrown under the bus. The child then becomes *the* center of your life as opposed to being *in* the center of your life.

I want to take a minute to explore the difference between being the center of attention as opposed to being *in* the center of our lives and attention. Our generation of parents has become imbalanced with the idea that we need to actively make childhood magical and special. This usually puts the child *at* the center of attention. All things revolve around the child. And it's this weird paradox because, yes, everything we do is for our children because they need us and we need to provide the structure and routine. I mean, before having a kid, I would not have driven around aimlessly for an hour and a half because someone fell asleep two minutes before I got to the house. Right?

We have a life with our kids but everything shouldn't revolve around the child. This puts them in a glaring spotlight that separates them from the family and community. One of the reasons baby wearing has historically been a thing and certainly come back into public favor is that wearing your baby allows you to move about your day *with* the baby. So the baby becomes part of your daily life. The baby is with you, taking part in your day, not separated off in this Land of Special Baby.

Once the child is *the* center of attention, a natural escalation happens. You may find yourself tripping over yourself to please the child, to make everything good and wonderful. There is a phrase I hear in at least 75 percent of my coaching clients. This phrase marks an issue so prevalent and yet so sneaky that most parents don't even realize it's an issue. That's right. Parents don't necessarily start working with me for this reason. And the minute we begin our work, this rears its ugly head, and I have to say, "Whoa! Let's start *there*."

Can you guess what it is?

My child won't let:

- me talk on the phone.
- me clean the house.

- my husband put her to bed.
- my wife sit at the kitchen table.

Those statements may seem silly to you. Or maybe you're like *Yes, I totally get that!*

This whole "My child won't let me" can be on the periphery or it can be a giant elephant in the room. Either way, it needs to be worked on. First, we do have to separate this out from what I call regular "won't let me." We are naturally curbed when we have kids. We can't always do the things we want to do when we want to do them. When our kids are little, busy, and needy, we need to be appropriately available to them. A crying infant won't "let you talk on the phone." A mom of a toddler can't always work out when she wants to. As a dad, you can't always sit and read a book when little dude wants to climb all over you and play. Your three-year-old probably won't "let you" take her out for a fancy six-course dinner or a three-hour Philharmonic performance. That's true.

But we also can't let the child hold the household hostage. That may sound like a harsh word if you're not in that situation. But based on my work, I'd say a lot of parents are very in it.

As I discussed in the last chapter, we simply must be the ones in charge. We are smarter and know more about how the world works. We understand the long-term consequences of our actions. Our little guys don't.

Styles of parental authority

In our modern parenting world we tend to see two polar opposite sides of a spectrum. We have the old-school "kids are to be controlled" type of parents. And we have the new-school "children are in control, loose boundaries, too many choices, lax-permissive" style. I consider myself and my parent coaching style to be a good mixture of both.

These differences largely correspond to *authoritarian*, *authoritative*, and *permissive* parenting styles. Often authoritarian and authoritative get confused, and they have become nearly synonymous. But they are not.

1. Authoritarian Parents: dictatorial or very rigid parents

The definition of *authoritarian* is "favoring or enforcing strict obedience to authority, at the expense of personal freedom."

Authoritarian parents believe that children are, by nature, strong-willed and self-indulgent. These parents value obedience to higher authority as a virtue unto itself. Authoritarian parents see their primary job as bending the will of the child to that of authority—the parent, the church, the teacher. Willfulness is seen to be the root of unhappiness, bad behavior, and in some cases, sin. Thus a loving parent is one who tries to break the will of the child. This is the "because I said so" kind of parenting.

2. Authoritative Parents: pragmatic or adaptable parents

The definition of *authoritative* is "able to be trusted as being accurate or true; reliable; commanding and self-confident; likely to be respected and obeyed."

Authoritative parents are also strict, consistent, and loving, but their values and beliefs about parenting and children are markedly different from authoritarian parents. Authoritative parents are issue-oriented and pragmatic, rather than motivated by an external, absolute standard. They tend to adjust their expectations to the needs of the child. They listen to children's arguments, although they may not change their minds. They persuade and explain, as well as discipline. Most important, they try to balance the responsibility of the child to conform to the needs and demands of others with the rights of the children to be respected and have their own needs met.

3. Permissive Parents

The definition of *permissive* is "allowing or characterized by great or excessive freedom of behavior; not obligatory; optional."

Permissive parents tend to avoid any confrontation or discipline, instead letting their children figure things out on their own. They often don't set any rules, boundaries, or expectations. There are usually two beliefs common in permissive parenting. One, the assumption that the child is capable of making good decisions. Or two, the assumption that good or bad, the child will learn through negative or positive consequences with little to no interference from the parent. The permissive style is how many of us parent in the first year or two, when the child almost certainly has inherent boundaries such as undeveloped gross motor skills.

The reason I'm clarifying these styles is that they come into play when we go back to that notion of governing in the zero to six years. And parenting style is going to be a theme throughout this book, so it's important you understand where I'm coming from.

How to apply parental authority

Words like *govern* and *power dynamic* can often be seen as authoritarian, and parents recoil from them. That is not how I'll be using the words or concepts. I mentioned my favorite parenting expert, Kim John Payne, in the introduction. The reason I'm so high on his concept of governing, gardening, and guiding is that it's beautiful—in reality, not just in theory. I intuitively used it in my own parenting. I've seen the results both professionally and personally in my own community. And it rocks.

If you lay the groundwork in the zero-to-six age range, the years to follow are wonderful. When the family's rules and boundaries are established early, you spend the following years enjoying your kids and cultivating a strong relationship. Think of now as the time to lay down the foundation. It won't always be this hard—once you put in the time solidifying that foundation. And as sweet and loving as they are right now, *wait*. Raising these little humans will get infinitely more interesting as their brains and bodies grow. You've been warned.

On the other hand, if you lay a shaky foundation, your parenting structure will need a lot of fixes later on. If you choose to not set any rules, boundaries, and expectations in the early years, you will have a very hard time setting them in the later years. What happens then is that when your child is six to twelve years and becoming so, so wildly interesting, you will then be stuck with governing. Which is a lot harder and much more unpleasant. When you are super firm with your boundaries early on, your child knows that you mean what you say. She learns that, yes, she can push limits, but you are right there, holding that "fence" in place. Which means in the next chunk of years, you can truly enjoy her personality and not be overly concerned about discipline, consequences, and your child's pushing your every button.

By governing and being more of an authoritative parent now, you get to spend the later years cultivating those seeds you sowed and truly have a blast "gardening" with your child.

In keeping with this govern, garden, guide model, I can safely say that most parents are trying to guide their little ones into the preschool years. This approach signals permissive parenting. And it can land you in a mess. Because if your child is doing his job and exploring all his limits and you are trying to guide him, you will learn quickly that your average three-year-old doesn't want to be guided. In case you haven't heard, he wants *to do it by himself!* Often with no clue how to go about whatever it is he's trying to do. This is totally fine if it's putting on his pants. But not so great if he wants to cross the street.

We also have to take a dip into actual brain development to see why trying to guide your preschooler may not work exactly as intended. In addition to that psychological process of individuation, we also have the pesky issue of your child's frontal lobes not being fully developed. We have two sides to the frontal lobes: one for thinking and reasoning, the other for social and emotional development. Both sides of the frontal lobes are interconnected, and together they are the driving force behind our ability to understand and reason, plan, and organize. They regulate our emotions and responses, and keep our impulses in check. The role of the frontal lobes is to direct the overall activity of the brain as a whole. Like the chief executive of a huge organization, they decide which ideas to run with, determine what your priority is at this very moment, and oversee the functioning of all the other areas of the brain. They give us the go-ahead to act, react, or not act at all.

The thinking and reasoning area tells us where we should be concentrating our attention, what we should remember, and when and when not to act.

The social and emotional area oversees our emotions, regulates our feelings, puts them into context, and helps govern our responses, while keeping a check on impulsive actions.

Hmm. Are you seeing the problem here? If you have ever spent or are currently spending time with your average three-year-old, you probably don't need any brain science to know that, yes indeed, our little guys have undeveloped frontal lobes and aren't equipped to make any kind of if/then decisions.

Over the next twenty years, the frontal lobes will continuously develop. Your child will begin to get long-term judgment and good decision-making, be able to understand ramifications of actions done or not yet done.

But it ain't happening right now.

Impulse control is *just starting* to develop around age four. I repeat: just starting.

All this means is that it's incredibly hard to "guide" children in life at this age. They are not physically capable of meeting us in the middle, here. Our collective expectations are way too high.

But also check this out. It's important. If we only try to reactively guide our children and don't give them our rules, boundaries, and expectations, then they don't know how to play this game of life. Imagine someone sitting you down to play a board game. There are no rules to start with, so you randomly move your piece. The other player gets mad. "That's not how you play!" You sit there totally befuddled and say, "What are the rules here?" The other player says, "You can figure it out. Explore. Have fun. I don't have to give you rules." So you move again and get yelled at.

Totally. Crazy. Making. Right?

I don't say *crazy making* lightly. It is psychologically unsafe for a child to live in a situation where she doesn't know the expectations. And the expectations should be set at a young age. This is a common mistake many parents make. They know, of course, that rules and expectations will have to be in place eventually, but they don't act soon enough. They attempt to parent the preschool years the same way they parented the early toddler years. It's apples and oranges. Still fruit but different. When these boundaries aren't established early, you can feel your parenting running away from you.

For now it's important to get philosophy out of the way. In real life, what served as a guideline can now be a roadblock. What served you in the first two years of life may not serve you the same way now.

All this talk is not meant to define you or how you parent. In fact, I want the opposite. Regardless of your parenting style (or lack thereof), my point is that what's most important is parenting the child you have, at whatever stage of development that child has reached.

Most often parents balk at the words *govern* and *authoritative*, so I really wanted to clarify that for you. Governing means setting rules and boundaries and expectations but doesn't have to look power-hungry and mean.

The Big Takeaway

Parenting philosophies are like birth plans. You can have your vision but then life may give you a totally different situation and you have to go with that. Do not be so tied to a philosophy that you miss the child right in front of you. I want you to understand why the best-laid plans in pregnancy, infancy, and the early toddler years may go haywire somewhere around the three-year mark. It's all good until it's not, and just like that Ferrari switching gears, you must as well.

I assure you, laying down this foundation early on will allow for more lax parenting down the road. Those easy bedtimes? The long conversations over a beautiful meal, one they eat? That idealized vision you had when you thought of parenting? It's coming! I promise. Just not yet. Now is the building phase. Make that foundation strong now so it stands the test of time.

CHAPTER 3

CONNECTION

Connection, connection, connection. It is the name of the game in parenting. Actually, in all our relationships. True connection—not just doing things together. You can be wildly connected with someone who is not in the room. And you can spend every minute of every day in the presence of someone and still be very disconnected. True connection is like being connected by heartstrings. It's more easily defined by what it's not. It's not teaching moments or being a mistake monitor. It's not judging. It's being very present and really seeing other people and loving them for who they are.

We have all had the experience of being with friends who are "talking to us" and simultaneously checking texts and/or social media, right? Yes. They are right in front of us. Yes. They are answering our questions and talking, but a big chunk of them is missing. We feel it. They are not connected to us even though all the external signs of connection are there. There's a missing internal presence. That's what I'm talking about.

This is what happens with our kids. When I bring up disconnection with families I'm working with, most parents are fairly incredulous. "Of course we're connected! Like, at the hip! This kid never leaves my side. I am always with him!" We spend so much time with our kids or so much of the day revolves around them that we sometimes make the mistake of thinking that we're connected when in fact there is a big disconnect happening.

Even if you are a parent who doesn't hover and helicopter, still—if you are the main caregiver—almost everything you do in a day is for your kids. At this young age, they are very needy and almost always need to be with us, even if playing. Oftentimes in a day, most parents doing child care have the desire to run from their kids, even if it's just a feeling. Like, *How can I get away for a minute?* We've all checked Facebook on the toilet with the door locked and little fingers trying to get under the door.

We've all read a children's book on autopilot. We've all uh-huh'd our kids when they want to show us something one. more. time. This is a version of disconnection.

Filling the emotional gas tank

When I talk about connection, I'm definitely talking about something different from physically being in the same room. I'm talking about the kind of connection that is heart and soul filling. In my work, I've always called it the emotional gas tank. Recently, I've seen a lot of different names for it: attachment tank, emotion bucket. I think it's even in the mainstream with folks saying things like, "My friends fill my bucket," after a good night out with friends and laughter. You know there are people who fill your bucket and there are people who drain every last drop. And lots of people in between.

Our kids operate best on a full emotional gas tank. You fill that tank through connection. The funny thing about filling that tank is that it usually doesn't take long and it usually doesn't take much. It just needs to be authentic and sincere.

Our little ones are so freaking sensitive, they can totally pick up on whether we are being authentic or not. They can totally tell when our minds are elsewhere and not focused on them and whatever we're doing with them.

Please understand I am not suggesting you focus only on your child all day, every day. We already are under super-duper über pressure, especially moms, to never, ever take our eyes off our kids. We already have this huge societal idea that we should be available and alert and planning freaking Pinterest birthday parties at all times. I am not suggesting that in the least. In fact, I'm suggesting you parent a whole lot less. I'm suggesting that you *do not* put so much focus on your child.

Toddlers and preschoolers are freaking awesome but they also won't fill your own bucket consistently. You need adult conversation and intellectual stimulation. You need physical intimacy and stress relief. If you're attempting 100 percent focus on your kids, you will crash and burn. Which will lead to feelings of "Fuck it. I deserve a break. I deserve to look at my phone while I'm coloring with this kid." It can turn into a wildly swinging pendulum. The goal is to not drain your own battery so you avoid having to shut down to recharge.

Our kids can tell when we're not really present, when we're not really connected. They can feel it, and it makes them hungry beasts. As much as I'm into the psychology of raising small humans, I'm also a businesswoman. And I like good ROIs (return on investments). I think of connection in these terms, as silly as that may seem. If you are giving 50 percent presence to your child 100 percent of the time, and that makes the child still 100 percent needy, it's just a bad investment of your time.

Whereas if you can be 100 percent present but for smaller chunks of time, and that fills your child's emotional tank and buys you some "off" time, that's a brilliant investment.

Did I lose you at the percentages? All I'm saying is this: concentrate your time with your little one. Their emotional gas tank will be full and they can cruise for a while without being needy or clingy. What we all tend to do is try to be available *all* the time and we fail, because we have to, we're human. Our kids end up getting crumbs of us and they *hate* that. So they act even needier.

All right then, how do you connect with your child without focusing on him all the time? Remember, kids don't need a lot to fill their tanks. They need a bouillon cube of your attention; it needs to be concentrated. They need to know they matter and not in a secondary way. But it really, truly only needs to be in small amounts!

If you are going to play with Play-Doh, do so 100 percent. If you are going to read a book, really read it and ask questions and talk about it. Mindfulness is all the rage these days. You don't have to go to a yoga studio or meditation retreat to be mindful with your child. Use your activities with your kids to practice. Try not to let your mind wander while working/playing with them. But honestly check in with yourself. How long is that focus sustainable for you? To honestly be present 100 percent? When a person begins meditating for the first time, it's suggested she start with three to five minutes! It's *that* hard to keep your mind from wandering.

Factoring in your tolerance for focus and how much time your child actually needs to get her tank full, I have found that twenty to thirty minutes is usually plenty in one sitting. That's enough for the child, but it's also when you will run out of steam for being super focused with what she is doing. That's when the holy-shit-I-can't-make-another-Play-Doh-snake starts to sneak in. Your to-do list starts to beckon.

That's when you call it quits. Anything after that point is

going through the motions. Again, please don't get me wrong here. A large portion of our interaction with our kids *is* going through the motions. Some of it just sucks. It's not possible to give 100 percent all the time. Our lives pretty much revolve around our children, but much of that time is spent doing the things we have to do—meals, scheduling, laundry, mistake monitoring, teaching. What I'm talking about is creating moments when you *are* 100 percent. That's what will fill their bucket.

My own kid was mind-numbingly into model trains for a good four years, starting at age four. Watching model trains is like watching grass grow. Of course, I loved watching *him* find so much joy, and so I would totally get into it. I had about a ten-minute tolerance for asking questions and be totally interested. But those ten minutes would fill his tank. My interest and my focus on those boring trains meant the world to him. He'd even sense when I'd had enough. "Okay, Mommy, you can do your work now." That's it! Tank full and I was released!

Now, if your child doesn't willingly let you go, how do you extricate yourself from the activity? Because once a kid has that focus and attention, most parents complain that they are now hostage to the activity. The child won't release the parent's focus and may cry or throw a fit. A large portion of my clients are terrified of this concentrated focus because they are afraid of what happens when they do want to call it quits and get back to what they need to do. "It's never enough. This kid wants more and more." Many parents report this feeling of running from their kids, which of course isn't true connection. They may dip into some focused play, but they largely try not to get too engaged because the child can't seem to get enough. You may hear "Read to me" and just know that means endless books and a fit if you try to limit the time or number of books. So you may resort to a push-off, like

> Sure.
> In a minute.
> When I'm done with x-y-z.
> Not right now, but later.
> I just read to you, I have to make dinner.

You may find that you do that to not get sucked down the needy-kid rabbit hole.

But listen! If you practice these concentrated connections and make them commonplace, your child will be *full* and you won't experience that neediness. If a child is super clingy and won't release you in a clean way, it means her tank has been drained into the negative. I know gas tanks don't work that way, so bear with me on my tangential analogy here.

Your child is experiencing an attention scarcity. So when she gets some attention, she is going to attempt to overfill herself. It feels *wonderful* to have your parents that present. It shines soul-filling light into their little hearts. They're not stupid: they want to hang on to that particular joy. It reminds me of one of my least favorite phrases ever: "Oh, he's just doing that for attention." Dude. Give him attention. Yes, I know at times kids will be over-the-top silly just to get laughs. However, if you find that your child always seems to be doing crappy things for attention, she may, in fact, just need more of this connection type of attention.

So this all takes practice for everyone to get acclimated. When your child knows that you will have to leave the connection activity but that there will be *more*, he is more likely to be peaceful when you extricate yourself. Remember toddler time, though. It works in very short increments, and the tricky thing about the emotional gas tank is that it's small. It doesn't take much to fill it, but likewise, it doesn't take much to empty it. Big emotions (like tantrums) will drain it, as will exciting outings like the zoo or children's museum. Believe it or not, playgrounds aren't that great a place to connect either. It's a wonderful activity and children need to be running around and playing. However, as we all know, most playground time is spent with the parent in protector mode and the child in free-play mode, which is fabulous but isn't filling the tank.

Activities for meaningful connection

Small emotions can fill your toddler's emotional gas tank in a manageable, digestible way. Here are some good connection activities:

Engaged reading. This usually excludes bedtime reading because, in reality, you are probably phoning these stories in. And that is completely fine; you're wiped out, your kid is wiped out, and bedtime stories function more as settle-down quiet time and a go-to-sleep cue. You can take some time during the day or waking hours to read. If your mornings aren't crunched and you have time, engaged reading is a wonderful way for everyone to ease into the day.

If you are a stay-at-home parent, you can have regularly scheduled reading time with your toddler. My son is older, so we have regularly scheduled game times; that way he doesn't try to randomly rope me into a long-ass Monopoly game. Toddlers *love* routine, so having a regularly scheduled reading time works wonders for filling that tank.

Play-Doh, artwork, coloring—any hands-on table/sit down work. While playing, be sure to verbally engage. "I'm making the longest snake in the world. What are you making?" "Let's make a snowman. Here's how to roll the dough into a ball." Playing with art supplies is a wonderful opportunity to teach colors and shapes, but be cautious not to turn it into a boring educational lesson. Kids can smell that a mile away. If you are tuning into your inner teacher, you will be less likely to be authentically connecting with your little one.

Chitchat. My niece and my mom actually came up with using that word. My niece never wanted to nap when my mom would be caring for her. So my mom would say, "Let's go lay down and just chitchat." My niece would always fall asleep, but it also became their thing. "Mem, can we go lay down and chitchat?" Our kids really want to converse with us and be part of our conversation. It's a part of why they interrupt us—to be included in all the talking. Unfortunately, because of the short amount of time they've been on the planet, they don't have *that* much to contribute to a conversation. But they *love* to talk with you. You can talk about favorite things, favorite colors, anything really. Usually when our kids are talking to us, we're doing other things, like cooking or driving, and we can't give them our full attention. Twenty minutes of superengaged conversation, all ears, fosters the sense that you like your child. I'll never forget one day, I told Pascal how much I like talking to him. He was astounded. "You like talking to me?" "Yes. I like hearing about what you think." "I thought you had to listen 'cause you're my mom." He was glowing. It was hilarious but it also made me pause. I think a lot of times we give off the unconscious vibe that we "have to" because it's our job, not because we enjoy it.

Movies and downtime. Watching a movie with your child can either be a fantastic break for you or it can be wildly engaging. I have no judgment about how you use screen time. If you are using it for a break, just know that and be clear with your child. Your child may have the expectation that you are going to sit like him, rapt with attention, enjoying each moment. You may have to vocalize that you are using this time as a break. You can say something like, "Yes, you can watch a show, but I need to do some things so I won't be watching with you." Simple and truthful. What you should avoid is telling your child that you two will watch a movie together and then sitting and "watching" but really scrolling your phone. Your little one won't miss a beat and will be resentful at having to compete for your attention. You can also use the movie for later chitchat, if you're not using it as a connection activity. "What's your favorite song in *Moana*?" "I love the part where blah-blah happens. What's your favorite part?" If you haven't picked up on the theme here, kids love discussing their favorite and their least favorite. They are all black-and-white thinkers at this age, so discussing the *best* and the *worst* is a big part of their little lives.

Cooking, helping in the kitchen, helping with chores. All of these should be a regular feature in your routine. Cooking at this age is more of a connection activity than a productive activity. If you're really trying to churn out a meal in a reasonable time frame, it's awesome to have your little one there helping and learning the kitchen ropes, but it probably won't be the best time for connecting with him. Baking is often better as a connection activity. With baking, there's usually more time to spend on the project, so there's less pressure on both of you. Baking also usually includes more action for the child—

59

dumping and stirring the ingredients, licking the spoon, and of course, waiting for a way more fun end product.

These are just a few examples, so feel free to do your own thing. The goal we're looking for here is engagement, a back-and-forth between the two of you. It should be open-ended without any pressure to actually produce anything (as in cooking and some art activities). It should be relatively distraction-free for both of you, so the engagement can really blossom without interruptions. You know it when you're in it because it also fills *your* cup/bucket/emotional gas tank. You feel like a stellar parent; it lifts you up rather than exhausting you.

How to peacefully finish connection activities

So now you've got a plan to sit with your kid to play with Play-Doh. You are so present you can't even deal and it's wonderful and it's all going great, and then you're done. You can feel your mind drifting, it's just not fun anymore, and really . . . lunch better be made soon or some little being is going to trip into hangry land (if you're not familiar with this term, it's the extreme anger brought on by being hungry; found in toddlers and adults alike). Your little one is being charming and you have sincerely had a wonderful time. Now it's time to pack it up, but little one is not having it. Whining escalates to crying escalates to throwing herself on the floor. Your connection has just been shot to hell. And this crap makes you wonder why you got the damn Play-Doh out in the first place.

Sound at all familiar?

The bigger question becomes, How do you end these connection activities peacefully? As I've mentioned, practice. It's going to take your child a while to get out of connection scarcity. Let's take this from the child's point of view. If you're like most parents, you've been phoning in a lot of potential connection activities (no judgment whatsoever: we all have done it). When you lock into true connection, of course your child doesn't want it to end!

(Bear in mind, I am always talking about your average, neurotypical child throughout this book. If your child has a diagnosis, connection activities won't necessarily play out like this.)

At first, you may have to do shorter but more frequent connections. This lets the child know that there is more coming. Once she is deeply assured that your glorious connection moments aren't scarce, she'll be more likely to let the present one go peacefully.

Another important part of this is that we're looking to get *you out of* the activity, not necessarily *end* the activity. You can say something like, "Okay. In five minutes, I need to do a little work on my phone. Would you like to make one last thing together?"

Five minutes go by.

"Okay! I need to do some work on my phone. You can keep playing while I do my work. We'll clean up in a little bit."

Now, it may seem and feel ridiculous to be breaking down something as a "Play-Doh playing moment," but there's a few very important messages being sent here. There's absolutely the connection, that's key. But there's also a subtle setting up for the beginning of independent play. Some kids play independently all on their own. And some kids need to be taught and sort of "unglued" from you. This is how you bridge your child from needing you for every little thing to playing independently.

There's also a huge parental self-care moment here. "I get my time too." Above, I called it "work on the phone." In reality, you can use that time to scroll social media or answer texts. In other words, it doesn't have to really be work. Wink, wink.

Focused connection versus multitasking connection

You can use this connection strategy in all different circumstances. We're looking for concentrated time for the myriad things you have to do. We now know that multitasking blows. As a parent, multitasking leaves you scattered and frazzled and pulled in a million directions. You often end up exhausted and unhappy with your results. That's a super common issue I hear among parents. If you feel like you're doing everything and yet not doing any of it well, it's time to slow down and stop multitasking.

I'm asking to you to play with your child and do nothing else but engage with her for that time, twenty or thirty minutes tops. Then take some time to go do your stuff. Just sit for a minute now and think about how playing with your child often feels. Sometimes it's unbearably boring, right? Your phone may be right there. You're secretly grateful for any notification because it gives your brain an excuse to do something besides, for instance, playing house, being directed by your three-year-old on what to say. Or you may keep popping up to add something to your list, throw in a load of laundry, put some dishes away.

That halfhearted play is almost never just play, so it's not this concentrated time we're looking for, right? It's scattered and your child doesn't feel that connection. Which is why you may have read this whole chapter thinking, "I play with my kid all the time and it's never enough."

A child who really feels that connection and knows more is coming will be satiated with that small amount. His tank is full and he can cruise on autopilot for a while. The younger the child, the smaller the tank, so be aware that you have to connect a little more frequently. Again, connection doesn't have to happen in big chunks. The average two-year-old may need frequent ten- to fifteen-minute segments every hour or two. A four- or five-year-old may only need a couple of twenty-minute chunks a day. When their attachment is super secure, they can learn to let go. If your child is whiny and clingy with you all the time, we look first to a secure attachment. That doesn't necessarily correlate to the amount of time spent with the child, as in time getting them ready to leave the house, time in the car, time while he's playing around you but not with you. We spend a *lot* of time with our kids, but that doesn't mean it's *connected* time. This is where that cliché came from: quality time over quantity. I homeschool my son. I am with him all the time, and entire days can go by without our actually connecting.

It can be very helpful to use the actual words *connection* and *disconnection*. "I feel very disconnected from you; let's sit and read a story so we can connect." This is a great tool as your kids get older. Having emotional language to wrap around feelings can be amazing! Your child will be able to articulate her feeling of disconnection, which can then be dealt with directly. When our kids can't articulate their feelings, they act them out. Which then can start a downward spiral because we attempt to address the symptom (crappy behavior) and not the root problem (feeling disconnected).

Before I wrap up this chapter, we must discuss *the phone*. Dun duh-dun dun. For most of us, it's the biggest means of connection and disconnection in our lives today. For busy parents, it can often be the one thing we get for ourselves. Texts feel immediate; we have to reply right now! It's so easy to want to check social media particularly if we just posted something super cute or particularly brilliant. I know. I'm guilty of it too.

But the phone can cause a huge disconnection in all our relationships but especially with our kids. Listen, I'm not this moral-high-horse person here. I may be one of the last people on the planet to think technology is not ruining us and that it's useful and good for our kids. I am not going to be like the whole internet telling you you're a bad parent for checking your phone. I do, however, think it needs to be time chunked out. I'll talk more about time chunking in the "Not Enough Time" chapter. Most parents I work with are just plain exhausted in addition to struggling with some behavioral aspect. We often work together to figure out where there are cracks and time is slipping away. The phone is a huge one.

And I'm going to point out the glaring elephant in the room that no one ever wants to talk about. Parenting is lonely. Especially if you're a stay-at-home parent. You love this kid to the moon and back, but conversing with a toddler all day is not fulfilling. Yes, parenting itself can be very fulfilling and I'm not suggesting otherwise. But the days can be long and boring and isolating. Reaching out on social media and texts can feel like your only connection to the outside world. However, when it comes to connection with our kids, dividing our attention between them and our phones can create that nasty cycle of not filling their tanks enough, so then they become even needier.

You may have even experienced your children swatting the phone or whining for you to put it away. Our kids know when we're not fully present for them. Again, I'm not coming down on phone use! You're a freaking warrior parent, I know you are. You get your phone time, for sure. My best advice, though, is that unless someone really needs you or you're expecting a text regarding plans for *that* day, put your phone in airplane mode for chunks of time lasting at least an hour. If you don't already do this, you will be shocked how much time you will get back. Texting, more than anything, drains our time and completely distracts us. Not just from our kids but from our everyday tasks. You can clean the whole kitchen pretty quick if your phone doesn't keep beeping for your attention. We are collectively all being pulled in too many directions and the phone really highlights that.

I started advising airplane mode to all my clients after I discovered in my own life how great it is.

You are already on call 24/7 for your little one. To make yourself available to anyone in your life, all the time, is crazy making. It slowly drains your energy from the important things and can totally exacerbate that needy feeling you get from your kids.

But check it out, because this is what it really comes down to: If you feel like everyone and everything is pulling at you, you will 100 percent feel your child is needier than they are. And you will not be able to give *them* the focus and attention they need. You will be frazzled and worn out.

Before we move on, remember this: occasional outbursts, superhigh-charged emotions, and epic tantrums are developmentally appropriate at two and three years old. *Occasional.* Not every day and certainly not more than once a day. If a child is constantly all over the map emotionally, we must look deeper. The behavior is just a symptom of something else happening and it largely starts with that connection.

The Big Takeaway

Connection is engaging with your child in a meaningful, heartfelt way. It's not teaching, being a mistake monitor, or directing the child what to do. You know it when you're in it because you feel like an excellent parent. When the connection with your child is disrupted (just like with friends and partners), you will see contentious behavior—snippy, cranky, and contrary. Before any correction can happen, connection must be present.

CHAPTER 4

PARENTS' SELF-CARE

Across the board, in my personal and professional life, I regularly see parental self-care thrown completely under the bus. I see marriages on the brink of failure because parents aren't attending to each other. It's all about the child(ren). In the long run, the family is what's going to sustain the child. To expect that a sole focus on the child can sustain the family is putting an awful lot of pressure on a little pair of shoulders. And of course none of us do that wittingly. But it does happen. We put all the energy and focus on the child and then are shocked when the household starts to crumble. We need to bring balance back to the family.

Self-care is often a misunderstood concept. Taking good care of yourself and your relationships requires good boundaries. Boundaries, and taking care of ourselves in general, go to hell in a handbasket when we're exhausted. And we are all exhausted. Like a lot.

For our generation of parents, in our particular society, it has become the norm to serve at the altar of parental martyrdom, boundaries be damned. There is a societal expectation for us to be everywhere, do everything, keep a careful eye at all times. There is a ridiculous belief that parents, particularly moms, should not let their children out of their sight. These expectations puts an enormous amount of strain on us as people. They can completely drain and exhaust us because we feel compelled to say yes to everything—every invite, every committee, every outing. This is why your boundaries have to be extra strong as a parent—to combat this pull that comes from all around us.

Again with this concept:

You must put on your own oxygen mask before assisting others.

You are a person who needs to attend not only to your child but to yourself, your marriage, and your adult relationships. Historically, mothers have been the people most in charge of the hearth and home and child-rearing. While there's been a wonderful shift toward papas being fully present in child-rearing, there's much data out there showing that women still bear a large portion of the child-rearing tasks. And historically, women have been worse at self-care than men. It's a broad generalization but true. This chapter is slanted toward mothers and women because that is definitely where I see the most troublesome gap, but these principles apply to *all* parents.

Please do not take this to mean I don't recognize how amazing dads are, how dads are fully taking part in the home and child-rearing. In an ever-increasing percentage, dads are the ones staying home or doing most care of the children. But in general, men have a tendency to have stronger boundaries. Men in general put up with far less shit than women. This goes for both in the home and out in the world. And again, we have a disturbing trend toward putting fault and onus on the mother if the shit hits the fan. If a child gets hurt or we see a viral video of crappy parenting, it's *almost never* "Where was that dad?" or "What a horrible father!" No, people comment about the mother and how she somehow screwed things up or did something horrific. In cases where the child is endangered with a caregiver, there's a huge outcry that the mom had the audacity to go to work and leave her child.

I want to explore how parenting got so out of balance for all of us. To do that, we must look back and see the historical roles we all played. For perspective, I'm fifty and my son is twelve. I'm telling you my age because not that long ago, family dynamics were much different. Not that long ago, when I was a kid, moms stayed home. Period. I clearly remember the frantic house-cleaning at about four in the afternoon. Not only would my mom have dinner started but I remember her sautéing onions to make the house smell as though she'd been cooking all day. How ridiculous is that, right? My dad came home at exactly the same time every day. He relaxed in His Chair (no one else was allowed to sit in that chair when he was around) and Lord help the child who disturbed his relaxing. Dinner was on the table by 5:30 p.m. Our sole job was not to bug him. Bedtime was 7:30 and my dad didn't read stories or help with bath time.

That sounds so archaic, doesn't it? So Archie Bunker (if you're old enough to get that reference). And my family wasn't out of the norm (although I'm sure there were families that didn't match this description).

Which isn't to say we didn't have fun with Dad. He was an avid gardener and we all spent hours in the dirt. We had family vacations and wrestling and he helped with homework, especially math. I remember his unending patience with my tears over long division.

The point I'm trying to make is that there's been a *huge* shift in the workload of men and women in the home in just one generation. It's fantastic, but bear in mind it's new. And there's a lot of spillover of expectations.

Bottom line: Please don't get your panties in a bunch while reading this chapter. I'm going to be referring a lot to the maternal workload, boundaries, and self-care. If you are reading this and it applies, please use it. If it doesn't, ditch it.

A real-life example

When I talk about self-care, I mean three kinds.

1. I mean *individual self-care*. Is each parent getting enough sleep? Downtime? Exercise? Is each partner eating well? Doing a hobby or activity that each truly enjoys? I'm talking fill-your-soul-cup kind of things.
2. I mean *parental self-care* in terms of your partnership. Is your marriage/relationship being cared for? I had an amazing therapist years ago who said a marriage is really three entities to care for: you, your spouse, and the third entity of the marriage/relationship. Are you caring for that third entity? This notion goes way beyond a monthly or even weekly date night. Are you making meaningful connections with each other?
3. And last, I mean *family self-care*. Is the family being tended to? As a whole? Does everyone in the family feel connected to one another? Are the things you value being put in the forefront or is everything getting lost in a scheduling shuffle?

Jim and Maya were an awesome couple I once worked with. They took their parenting super seriously. They read and researched and had the sincere desire to be the best parents they could possibly be. They came to me because their third child, Julia, was having legendary tantrums at least four or five times a week. Tantrums that would bring the house to a halt and everyone in it to their knees.

When I start working with a family, I ask them, of course,

what they think the big looming problem is, and then I ask them to walk me through a typical week. Here's why. The big looming problem is often not the actual problem. Your child's crazy behavior—fighting you at bedtime or refusing to eat or whatever big looming problem is at hand—is usually a symptom of a deeper problem. Not necessarily something impossible or huge, but almost always something more somewhere. We have to look for the cause, for the "disease" if you will. If we only treat the symptom, the problem will return. Sure, I have a lot of tips and tricks for de-escalating tantrums and dealing with general problematic behavior, but we always have to dig a little deeper if we want a permanent fix. It's one of my frustrations with a lot of the parenting advice out there. They are Band-Aid fixes, attempts to fix the symptom, and the real problem is never addressed.

Jim and Maya had barely walked me through one typical day and I could already smell trouble. They have three kids, and those kids were overscheduled to the hilt. With a divide-and-conquer strategy, Mom and Dad literally spent their entire day carting their kids from activity to activity. Maya would take one kid, Jim would take the other two. The adults hardly ever spent any time with each other. They hardly ever spent time as an entire family. The kids' calendars were so completely full, they often grabbed dinner in the car or from the drive-through. Even at night, they had a sort of rotating bed schedule. There were four beds, but no one ever slept in the same bed, with Jim and Maya sort of sleeping with a different kid each night. Not only was their sex life nonexistent, it seemed like they'd never get it back.

Now, I happen to be a big proponent of cosleeping—*if and only if* it's what you want to do. And *if* it's working for the whole family, not just one or two of you. You and your children can sleep wherever you want, but in Jim and Maya's case this approach wasn't working for their whole family. First, it wasn't working for their marriage. Your relationship matters the most, and parents are sometimes shocked when I say this. We've gotten ourselves twisted into thinking that the child is what matters most. The child is part of a family, and you and your spouse are the basis of the family. Therefore, your relationship has to be solid, because it is the foundation on which everything else is built! This also goes for the single parent, perhaps even more so. If you're single, your self-care becomes even more important since you're pulling double duty.

Sometimes my job seems like it edges into marriage counseling, but this is really part and parcel with parenting counseling. If you do not take care of yourself and your relationships and you focus only on your children, you are a parenting martyr. And believe me, you will burn out. Or worse, you will find your marriage crumbling.

A big problem today is that parents are using their love and their marriage as a crash pad at the end of the day. Your love, your relationship should be the umbrella that protects the family. And that takes some work and attending to.

Many couples treat their marriage as "locked in." It's a given, so it can be ignored. "We agreed to be in this together, she knows I love her, so I don't have to attend to this." They rely on their love only when they're burned out. Their expressions of love (verbal or physical) are squeezed in when everything else is done. When you put your relationship in the forefront, your child will feel the love. Like an umbrella, it will protect you during challenging times.

Yes, at this age most kids are incredibly needy. As they get older and older, you will find more and more time for yourself, more and more downtime. But in these first six years, you have to be fairly brutal about carving out time for yourself, your relationship with your spouse/partner, and the family as a whole.

One of the things I usually ask parents is what they'd like their lives to look like; what's their vision? We all have one, and largely our feelings of parental failure arise because our vision and our reality are not matching up. I ask this question for two reasons. One, to make sure they're being realistic about life with kids. And two, because often we envision a life with our family and then we, largely unconsciously, go and do things that work against that vision.

Throughout our initial conversations, I kept picking up this thread that both Jim and Maya were craving more family time. They were craving slower days, a more relaxed existence, more connection with each other and as a family. They especially treasured food, both the time spent creating meals and the time spent together eating. Jim and Maya were caught in a classic parenting trap: putting all their focus on the children and none on the family. To be fair, they carved out a date night every week and a half or so, but Jim's big complaint was that they talked only about the kids. Maya's big complaint was that they never had enough downtime. She loves to bake and cook with the kids. She loves slow days where there's time for baking, art, and snuggles. Ultimately, they needed to let go of some of the activities for the kids. Jim and Maya were on the busy treadmill that closely ties into a parental anxiety treadmill. "We're not doing enough, so we must do more and more."

Fuel that with a dash of social media insecurity (trying to keep up with all the cool things in your newsfeed, which we all are susceptible to) and an idea that busy is good, and you have a recipe for disconnection. This family had themselves so overbooked, they could barely breathe, let alone connect. Julia was being pulled along on the busy train, which often happens with third kids. With a first child, we all have time and we're so careful about everything, making sure their little lives have everything and are perfectly balanced. And then by the third or fourth child, you are so busy with whatever all the older kids have going on, the youngest often gets pulled along. We know that the youngest is often exposed to movies and books that you wouldn't have dreamed of exposing your first to. In moderation, this relaxing of control is sort of what makes younger siblings so awesome. They are usually way more chill than the first child and they're masters at working the system and working the game of exhausted parents. So don't feel like you messed them up. Chances are you've given them a valuable gift.

With Jim and Maya, we had to really work on why they were creating the opposite of what they actually wanted. If they really wanted more downtime, why did they keep overbooking the kids? We'll cycle back to this question in the "Parental Anxiety" chapter. For now, suffice it to say that that was definitely part of the problem. But the other part was not giving any weight to the family as a whole, not giving any attention to their marriage. Jim and Maya were completely disconnected from each other. So naturally, the whole family was feeling disjointed and disconnected. And little Julia, being as sensitive as only toddlers can be, was picking up on everything. She was being rushed through transitions, and boy howdy, do little ones need *slow* transitions. Her epic meltdowns were starting to make sense.

We as a culture are obsessed with being busy. Stay busy! Stay active! Do more! And this obsession is rampant in parenting. Think about this for a minute. How often do you hear these words and how often do you say them?

You run into someone you know, it could be anywhere:

"Hey! How are you?"

"Oh! So busy!"

Right? Busy as a feeling. How are you? *I'm busy.* That's not even the right answer to "How are you?"

As our sessions continued, it also became apparent that the two older boys were pretty entitled and demanding. It particularly bothered Jim, who worked outside the home. Maya, staying home, was more in the thick of it. Sometimes it's hard to see a problem that needs attention when we're drowning in it. It took Maya a minute to see that she had put herself at the kids' beck and call. And as it goes with the power wand, once the kids have it, they run with it.

When all our focus, no matter how loving and well-intentioned, goes to the children, this dynamic gets created. If a child is at the center of everything we do, how can that child not start to feel like she is indeed the center of everything? If we don't carve time for ourselves and our relationships, our children simply grow up expecting us to be there for their every whim. When we don't emphasize the family as a whole over the individuals, then the child will simply learn that his individual needs come first and he will act accordingly, entitled and demanding.

How to tell if you need to spend more time on self-care

So you can see, self-care is about more than downtime, date nights, and mani-pedis. It's also about children understanding on a very deep level that they are a part of something. Something that matters to all of us as humans. When we know we count, we matter, and we are a part of something bigger, our behavior changes.

There's an African proverb that says, "A child not embraced by the village will burn it down to feel its warmth." I first saw this quote in conjunction with a school shooting. I also think it applies to less extreme situations. If a child doesn't understand that he's part of a bigger entity, the family in this case, that child will attempt to disrupt the family dynamic until he gets the human warmth he is so desperately craving.

It made me think of Julia and her crazy meltdowns. Listen, we *know* we love our kids beyond measure. And even without our catering to their every whim, our lives revolve around them. But Julia wasn't getting a deep sense of family. She was being pulled in eight different directions at light speed. Her wild fits were a call for attention, a "burn the village down to feel its warmth." She would literally hold down the house with her larger-than-life tantrums. We've already talked about this in the "Boundaries" chapter, where maintaining boundaries can certainly nip everyday toddler behavior in the bud before the power dynamic takes off in a weird direction. But Julia's behavior had given "holding hostage" a new meaning; it was definitely above and beyond the "normal range" of toddler behavior.

If you feel like you have a similar situation going on and you know it's not just boundaries that have gotten out of whack, you have to ask yourself this: Why would my child hold me hostage? For what gain? What is she trying to tell me?

Kids act out. Acting out gets a bad rap. It shouldn't; it literally is them acting out their feelings because they don't know how to articulate those feelings. The feelings are either too big, too overwhelming, or too complicated for them to be able to talk about them. When you are getting big behavior, there's a big reason behind it. True, there's always the possibility that your child is simply being a pain in the ass. But you in your parent heart usually know when the cause goes deeper. I honor that intuition and you should as well.

If Julia had grown-up words, they would probably have been along the lines of "Everyone *stop*. Slow down! I'm little. I need cuddles and time. I want to dress myself and pick my own clothes, but we are in too much of a hurry. Eating in the car feels yucky. I want to sit and eat my food slowly with all of you around me. Because you are my everything and I want to feel that love."

I mean, maybe not exactly those words, but something pretty close. Even harder to articulate is a *sense* of something being wrong but not even knowing what that is.

The very first thing we worked together on was that slowing down. Jim and Maya decided that Sundays would be an activity-free day. Whether you follow a formal religion or not, there's something to be said about the olden days when Sunday was a sacred day. It used to be that stores weren't open and you couldn't buy liquor and usually someone held a big family dinner. In my family, we went to one of my grandmas. To this day, I can remember the smell of her house.

Organized sports often now fill Sundays. Shopping and running errands. And, yes, I understand that sometimes that's the only possible day to do these things. I'm not suggesting everyone take Sundays off, but the important thing here is to *create the life you envision*. If you envision days in the kitchen, passing down your grandmother's spaghetti sauce recipe to your kids (the one that takes nine hours to cook), baking, and generally bonding in the common cooking space, then you will have to create that.

It's tough for most parents to become aware of the hard truth—and then to sacrifice something in that busy zone. It was extremely hard for Maya to think about giving up some of her kids' activities to create that Sunday space. It might sound easy, but she grappled with it in a way I think we all do. "What if they're missing out on something? What if they hate this and are mad at me for giving up their soccer? What if they don't get a soccer scholarship because I kept them home on Sundays instead of their playing their sport?" That may sound absurd, but don't laugh, that's a legit fear of parents today.

We had to really work around her feelings about this. Which incidentally brings us back to something I mentioned in the introduction: if you have some unhealed childhood wounds, they are going to affect your parenting. This was a perfect case in point. Maya had been adopted. She hadn't done all the healing work she needed to do. She was caught in this spinning web of having to be the perfect mom. The perfect mom for her was providing her child with all the opportunities she could possibly think of. We spent some time pulling that apart, and she realized that the best thing she could for *herself* was to give her kids that feeling of roots and tradition. Maya began to spend Sundays cooking and passing down her favorite recipes from her mom. Time to just be with the kids in the kitchen, baking and cooking, laughing and talking. Jim would take that time to do yard work, with which the kids would help.

It honestly took a month before they could make that Sunday space happen. Once they did, the changes were instant. The kids could move between the kitchen and the yard work. Each of them got some sibling alone time, some alone time with each parent. The connection Maya and Jim had with the family was incredible. Talking to them that week was joyous. They were both overflowing in their love for the family they've created. Which of course was immediate feedback for them and encouraged more changes. It's not often you get that kind of immediate feedback, but it's so cool when you do.

That first Sunday night that wasn't filled with busy, Jim and

Maya stayed up together, totally jazzed, plotting out how to keep this connection going and bring it into other days of the week that were more stressed for time. The kids all went to bed easily. And Julia didn't have a meltdown—not just that day but for almost a week. Her tantrums became a marker for the family connection. Maya and Jim were able to track when the busy got out of control. Sure enough, Julia would fall out, and they knew it was time to scale something back. They also were connecting between themselves—yes, about the kids, but not over a laundry list of what the kids needed. They were plotting their *family life* and it went so much deeper than who is driving which kid to what activity.

This is an important theme for me throughout this book. Think back on your childhood memories. Was it sports games you remember vividly? Was it special events? Disney? Most likely not. Our softest, most beautiful memories are in those loving family moments. Your dad showing you how to cut with a big knife. Your mom teaching you how to make spaghetti sauce. Those are the best memories we can give our kids. They will remember the connection.

As Maya Angelou said, "I've learned that people will forget what you said, people will forget what you did, but people will never forget how you made them feel."

Most important, Jim and Maya came to realize how their relationship was so very vital to the health of their family. Keeping themselves connected and cared for was a trickle-down economy for the kids. That's the glue that holds the family together. Staying connected as parents, people, and lovers has magic. At the very least it gives you a united front so you don't get any of the nonsense kids can pull when parents aren't in sync. You know what I'm talking about, because we all did it to our parents too.

I detailed Jim and Maya's story because too often we think our kids are being shitty because that's just how they are. Or we honestly don't even know why; it can seem unexplainable. There's some developmental wonkiness that happens for sure in their little exploding brains and bodies. But we also want to look for a root cause. Parental self-care is more than just taking care of yourself. It's creating that village vibe so that our kids feel a deep connection and love within that circle.

Alone time

But hey now! Did I just utter the words "taking care of yourself"? Yeahhhh, let's dig into that one now. There's family care and relationship care, but what about you parents individually?

Are you and your partner both getting enough time alone? With friends? Are you sleeping well? Exercising?

Typically this is where moms are weaker. And even if you have nontraditional parent roles—dad stays home while mom works, two moms, two dads, single mom, single dad, maybe you're grandma or auntie or polyamorous or whatever—this applies mostly to females because females are historically shittier at self-care than males. Do some males suck at self-care? *Yes.* But in *general*, females suck more.

I am also a mom. I have friends. And I work professionally with couples. And without a doubt it is typically women who take the brunt of the self-sacrificing. Sometimes for the first two years it really is because mom is nursing and the baby won't take a bottle.

Even in homes where the parenting roles are nontraditional, usually it's still moms remembering and sending out birthday cards, making appointments, doing many of the little tiny things that keep a household running. Again. If you are a dad and doing all of this, you are awesome. Then pay close attention here as well.

Remember when I said your marriage and/or the family connection is a trickle-down economy, it flows down to the kids? There's actually one level higher and that's you, the individuals. Are you caring for your own needs?

Making time for self-care in the first five years of your child's life is brutal. You are underslept, for starters. The first year is a blur as you and this new human figure each other out. There always seems to be something. I see parents just not taking care of themselves because they are completely burned out. They have no time and even less energy to care for themselves. They often end up in a fight because one parent typically is better at self-care than the other.

The most common scenario (and again, not being sexist, but in the large majority of couples I work with, this is the dad working outside the home, largely responsible for finances, and the mom staying home or working part time from home) goes like this: The working parent gets home. The stay-at-home parent is still home. Both are exhausted. The working parent needs a minute to relax after work. And so does the stay-at-home parent, who has also worked his or her balls off. Both need a break, but neither gets one. I literally just worked with a couple on this issue. Dad was the out-of-home worker; he'd get home and need a little bit of time for reentry into family life. Mom was going a tiny bit crazy because she'd been home with a one- and a three-year-old all day. She expected him to come home and immediately take over kid duty. He expected to come home after a hellish commute and to relax for a little while. They both needed a break, and both are right to need that break. So what were they supposed to do?

This is up to you guys to strategize with each other. First thing, however, is to recognize that *you both need a break*. Most likely, only like a half hour. But if you each don't take that time, you will be resentful of the other. And being resentful is a slow burn to relationship hell.

Over the years, this has become truly a common scenario I hear again and again, and each couple handles it differently. I'll give you a small list to help you brainstorm with your partner.

- I've worked with a few dads whose idea of relaxing was video games. All they needed was a half hour of video gaming and they were good to go and be Super Dad for the rest of the night. Since there was a time limit on it, one mom was okay with this. But the minute Dad took over, Mom was out the door for a yoga class.
- Another family decided that damn all the warnings, Dad could game with his kids and teach them the Jedi ways of the joystick.
- For another family, Mom worked outside the home and Dad stayed home. They agreed to meet at a playground. Dad would have the kids there, Mom would come after work. The kids would play and the adults had a park bench reconnection. Obviously, not every day but often enough that resentments didn't build.
- Yet another family, with both parents working, hired a regular sitter for an hour at that time. The sitter would often have the kids out of the house or in the tub, so Mom and Dad could get home, get dinner started, and decompress for a bit before taking on parenting duty.
- One mom I worked with was just drowning in perfect parenting. Nothing she did was just for her well-being. Even showering was an ordeal. Her husband would come home

82

and try to give her a break but her little boy would go crazy trying to find her when she attempted a mom-escape to another room. Finally, we figured out that Mom just had to walk out the door. She'd go for a brisk twenty-minute walk and come home rejuvenated. It was easier for her husband to take over dad duty when she actually left the house.

Every family is different and all the details will be different. The larger picture is, How can you both claim a little time during that clusterfuck hour? That time when someone is getting home from work, dinner needs to be made, and it's the witching hour for your kids. Just being aware that you both need a break can be helpful. I've worked with couples who both get resentful because they each feel their particular job is the more important one so they should be the one to get the break. The parent who works outside the home needs to decompress, and the parent who works in the home needs to decompress, and if you both work outside the home, you both need to catch your breath. Knowing that can go a long way to helping you claim some time.

Again, I totally understand that these are the needy years. I understand that it's not easy to carve time for yourselves, but it's vital. As I've said before, you must put on your own oxygen mask before assisting others. Not only is this key to not burning out, losing patience, and getting resentful, there's an additional bonus of modeling self-care to your children. There's a beauty in your children's seeing you take time for yourself. *It is not selfish.* We know there's a huge problem with entitlement in the current generation. In general, we're seeing more and more of our youth expecting the world at their feet without their having to do too much. If you are completely on all the time for your children and don't take care of yourself, that's what they learn. You have to remember they are in constant learning mode. We are constantly teaching others (and not just our kids) how to treat us. If you go and go and go and create no space for yourself, your children will learn that. And they will grow up thinking that's how moms or dads are. So modeling good self-care has way more benefits than just for you.

But let's get back to you because that shit is indeed very important. And fun.

Do you have a hobby or interest that takes you out of the house? Something that has nothing to do with parenting? I totally understand if you love crafting things for your littles or love to bake. What I'm looking for, though, is something outside that. Something that allows you to interact with other grown-ups and *not* talk about your kids. If you don't, think really hard about what you could do.

Or even, the next time you strike up a conversation with another parent in a group or a park, see if you can have a conversation not about your kids and their poop and their sleep. (Is it not unbelievable how much we can all talk about our kids' poop? Like *Who am I? I used to be cool!*) I'll never forget the first time another mom did this to me. We were at a playgroup-type thing and this vibrant mom comes up to me and says, "Hi! Are you reading anything good right now? I'm reading the best book!" And, OMG, shocking, it *wasn't even a freaking parenting book.* I was, like, speechless. I got home and immediately went to the library to get a crappy fiction book. I had totally forgotten that I get to read nonparenting books too! It was so refreshing, I also snagged her phone number. I wanted this woman in my life. We are best friends to this day and we try really hard to steer away from conversations about our kids. We are people too! Dammit.

When we turn our interests and conversations away from

parenting, even for a short time, the payback is huge. We get our souls filled. Which in turn makes us better parents. Our current media messaging and in fact our societal message is that we have to be *on*, parenting every moment of every day. That's not only exhausting, it's unrealistic *and* bad for our kids.

Remember the mom I just spoke about? The one who had to leave the house and go for a twenty-minute walk? Well, I gave her additional homework. She was to use those walks to think about something she'd like to do that had nothing to do with her little one. At first, all she could think about was things that somehow related to her child or the household. Yes. We'd all love extra time to finish laundry. And I ask many parents what they'd do if they had an extra hour just to themselves. And you would not believe how many say, "Do laundry." And I get it. It can feel really good to have a major task finally done. But my friends, you have to really think about this. If that's your answer, you may be drowning in parenting. For real.

A couple of weeks later, after doing this homework, she was tearful. "I forgot *me*. I forgot who I was. What I love. I love my little boy but I forgot about me." *Bingo.* She walked and walked and walked every day, and it took a while but at last she remembered the things she loved to do, just for herself.

Sleep as self-care

Do you sleep well? Do you get to bed at a good bedtime and wake feeling at least partially refreshed? Oh, man, I know we as parents are the legions of underslept. Yes, there will be horrible nights of catching puke and cleaning blow-out diapers. There will be nights of soothing a teething child or a kid screaming with growing pains in his legs. I understand that completely.

However, you have to think of sleep as an actual nutrient. When we consistently go without enough sleep, everything suffers: our mood, patience, coordination, ability to stay focused and organized. As the people in charge of our little guys, we all need to do better. Getting enough sleep is the best thing you can do for your parenting.

It is hard to do, I know. We have such limited time in a day, and often it all just gets away from us. It's so easy to stack our endless tasks and chores for "after they go to bed." Which often leaves us staying up too late. Or the kids are finally in bed and again you collapse in front of mindless TV, because you so desperately need the mind-numbing downtime. Sleep so often feels like a waste of time when we have so much more to do at the end of the day. One thing I've discovered both personally and professionally is that getting up early is far more useful than staying up late. You may already know this. Many, many parents get up super early to enjoy their coffee *alone*, eat their food *alone*, journal, work out, or just enjoy the early-morning solitude. You, of course, don't have to do this. It's just an idea to keep in your pocket.

When I started working with Molly and David, Molly was struggling miserably with mornings. The kids would get up before her and she would spend a few extra minutes in bed, going through Facebook. She wasn't a morning person, and having four kids under the age of six, she barely had even a moment to herself. This was her "Fuck it. I deserve this time." The only problem was that by the time she got up, the kids were psycho. They were hungry and she'd missed that window of feeding them before they went crazy.

We spent a lot of time finding pockets in the day when Molly could get some downtime. Often it really only takes about twenty minutes a couple of times a day to fill your own cup. We worked on organizing her chores and endless laundry; we worked on getting the kids to help more. Even little, little ones can be responsible for small chores. Molly and David needed some more connection time that didn't involve binge-watching TV. We worked on her self-care throughout the day so she didn't have to crash into a stubborn "*I deserve this!*"

And for Molly, downtime was specifically looking like this: exhausted at the end of the day, but knowing she and David needed time together, they routinely would sit and watch *The Walking Dead.* Which is fine but not really true connection. They would—we all know how it happens—end up watching several episodes. Thanks to Netflix we no longer have to wait a week to see what happens after the cliff-hanger, right? And I love that. Except when it takes over. Molly and David were staying up too late with a fairly empty activity. I'm not saying you can't watch your programs. I am saying that our time and relationship have a sort of nutritional value to them, right? Really connecting with our loved ones is as beneficial as eating kale. Watching four episodes and staying up too late is like eating all the Halloween candy in one sitting.

Molly still wasn't feeling like she got enough "me time," so in the morning she would lounge in bed for a few minutes, scrounging for that needed break. *Which she should indeed get.* The timing however, was wrong. Early morning was a vital time of day when her absence would set the house up for disaster. A mere twenty to thirty minutes in bed made the rest of her day a living hell.

Molly and David committed to watching one episode together and absolutely making room for connection. Some nights it was hard and they literally had to set a timer. "Thirty minutes of connection. Let's go." Kind of like, hurry up and relax. They both committed to being in bed by ten thirty, eleven o'clock at the latest. And feeling rested, Molly was able to get up earlier than the kids, have her time to herself, and start the day ahead of the curve.

If you routinely shave hours off your sleep, you will not be your best parenting self. It's hard to wrap our heads and routine around this notion, but *you are doing something when you sleep.* I know it feels like you're not, with the endless to-do list staring you in the face. I know that. But you are regenerating your body, your brain, your patience, your stamina. Parenting is a slow-paced marathon, man. You have got to pay attention to replenishing your system and going at a steady, even pace.

Movement as self-care

Last, a huge component of your self-care is making sure you move your body in some way. Do you move your body? This could mean using an exercise video, taking a walk, running, going to the gym or a group class, or taking a bike ride. It doesn't have to be long or formal or make you burn a thousand calories. Just something that moves your body in a way you enjoy. A good rule of thumb is getting yourself out of breath a few times. Again, this doesn't have to be formal. And for the love of all that is holy, it isn't and shouldn't be about maintaining a certain weight or body ideal. This is about *taking care of your whole body, your mind, and your spirit.* I'm pretty sure I don't have to tell anyone the positive effects of movement. For you, the parent of little ones, I think stress relief is probably top of that list. Next is an endorphin rush. Man, do you need those endorphins.

It can be a challenge to fit this self-care in, especially if you want to return to a regular exercise routine you had before having kids. You most likely won't have the time right now to do the kinds of exercise you did then. Your exercise will be different but it's still vital. There are many options now for moving. Tons of "fit moms" on Instagram and YouTube are sharing playground workouts, simple exercises you can do with your kids. Guess what? You don't need weights, just throw that little one on your back and bust out some high-quality squats and lunges.

Give physical activity some focus and don't be shy: it's wonderful to do it with your kids or in front of your kids. Something a lot of parents don't realize is that kids don't do what we say, kids do what we do.

Modeling self-care

Modeling self-care is a truly amazing gift you can give your children! Without saying a word, you are showing them how to care for themselves, how to set boundaries so they're not draining themselves dry in giving too much. Taking care of you shows them that you respect and love yourself. Is there anything better than that? Particularly, we need to show our little girls. While it's true of both genders, little girls tend to feel a greater societal pressure with body image, beauty, and skewed boundaries. Modeling self-care for them is vital so they have a strong base of self-love for later in the preteen and teen years. Do you prepare wonderful food for your kids and find that you don't sit to eat it? Do you grab their crusts and fruit peels, not making time for yourself to eat? Do you grab energy bars on the go and eat in the car? They are watching and learning. My wish for you is to take care of yourself because you deserve care. But it's also important to remember what we are teaching. Because we are always teaching. These little suckers are always watching.

The concept is the same for our little boys but in a slightly different way. In a general sense, our boys and men get a societal message that they can carry any burden, that they are not as emotional as girls and don't need downtime. We collectively expect them to have strong emotional shoulders and to not show too much if they are experiencing overload. Taking time to care deeply for yourself, admitting to yourself that you need downtime can go a long way in helping our boys see that you don't always have to "suck it up" or, in one of my least favorite phrases ever, "be a man."

What ends up happening to most parents is that we tend to put ourselves last. Often that's just part of the deal. What happens then, though, is that your self-care tends to be left for that crash pad at the end of the day, instead of being an umbrella to protect you through the day. And what does that self-care look like? Mindlessly scrolling Facebook and Instagram, bingeing on Netflix, maybe drinking a glass of wine too many. This type of self-care is like eating a two-pound bag of M&M's: it feels okay in the moment but makes you feel like shit in the end. If you leave self-care until the end of the day, you will have crappy self-care. And crappy self-care usually means that you're doing something that actually isn't very good for you. A big clue is if you find yourself saying the words, "Well, I deserve . . ."

True self-care is proactive, not reactive. And it's not all massages, mani-pedis, or retail therapy. True self-care sometimes means being brutal with your time. It's getting up early to move your body. It's making yourself shut down all devices at a reasonable time. It's getting to bed religiously at an earlier time than seems feasible. It's living with a less than perpetually clean house so you can carve some time for yourself.

I've used this phrase several times about parental self-care. Your marriage, your mental health, your family love should not be a crash pad at the end of the day. It should be an umbrella protecting the family all the time. Too often, when we keep ourselves so busy and use that care as a crash pad, we crash and burn—if not every night when the kids go to bed, then certainly over time. The biggest problem with this crash pad is that you're exhausted by the time you hit it and totally out of juice, never mind creative thinking. And forget sex. If you can flip your self-care to become an umbrella that protects you, your relationships, and the family, you can be more proactive throughout the day, when you have the energy to maintain boundaries and think creatively. When you have the time and energy to slow down to toddler time.

The Big Takeaway

You count. You matter. Not just as a parent but as a human. If you consistently put your child first, you will crash and burn. Good self-care isn't just about self-preservation or being the best parent you can be, it's also about modeling self-care for your child. And doing away with much of the child entitlement that's so prevalent today.

CHAPTER 5

NOT ENOUGH TIME

In the last chapter we talked about self-care. Making time for self-care can make parents want to cry because they already feel overwhelmed with not enough time. I'd say one of the most common complaints of parents everywhere is not enough time. This chapter is going to be slightly different from the others because it's actually a mini-course I give to my clients. I call it the Magical Cataclysmic Time Expander. It's a humble name.

Seriously, though. It's a mind-blowing concept called the Pareto Principle. Once I heard about it and applied it, my time shifted; I literally have more time. I wrote my experience down to give to other moms in my community. And then, knowing it changed everything for *them*, I started giving it to clients. I subsequently learned that there are many books written on this principle. I know you don't have time to read another book, so I'm using this seven-step exercise to highlight what I've found.

I know what you're thinking, because I would be thinking it too. I hate books that make you do exercises. I never do them. I kinda sorta do them in my head. So if you're like me, don't do that. These steps can seem disjointed as you're doing them. That's okay, it's a puzzle that will all come together at the end, don't worry!

But you have to actually do it. This is not time management bullshit you've read a million times already. This is not life balance (there is no such thing). It won't take long but, *but* you do need to fully commit. If you don't give this good attention, you'll keep drowning in lost time. So let's go.

Step One—The Pareto Principle

I'm going to assume you are a bit like I used to be. Feeling like there's never enough time, right? Drowning in my twenty-four hours every day, constantly stretched too thin. Doing a hundred things and not one of them really well.

The Pareto Principle can change your life. Above all, like Maya and Jim in the last chapter, remember: *This is your life to design.* You really do get to design your life, but first you must figure out where your time and energy are going and if you're using them well. That's what we'll be doing here!

I'm going to use my own experience throughout since it *still* blows my mind how great this method is. First let me say this: A lot of people assume that as a successful author, I'm very rich. I am not. I work full time. I do have the luxury of making my own schedule, but I am a living, breathing full-time mom. I don't have hired help. I regularly get behind my own eight ball and am not immune to all the parenting pitfalls. Just want to put that out on the table. I've done this mini-course myself, many times over. And I swear, I get three more hours to a day.

This too can be yours, it's that magical.

First the concept.

It takes a minute to really get it. And then once you get it, you still have to walk around with it marinating in your brain to, like, *get it.* It's mind-blowing, though, once you do.

It's an economic and statistical concept called the 80/20 principle.

Twenty percent of your energy output yields 80 percent of

your results. Let that sink in for a minute. Only 20 percent of what you do in any given situation is responsible for 80 percent of the results.

The concept came from the Italian economist Vilfredo Pareto, who noted back in 1896 that 80 percent of the land was owned by 20 percent of the population. His original observations were applied to population and wealth: 20 percent of the people have 80 percent of the income. But then somewhere along the line, people started to figure out that this ratio applies through many different systems. Check this out: In software, fixing 20 percent of the most reported bugs eliminates 80 percent of the errors/crashes. In athletic training, 20 percent of the exercises have 80 percent of the impact. In gardens, 20 percent of the plants will produce 80 percent of the produce. And more recently, this idea has been used to sharpen productivity to the most effective level. Twenty percent of your time is giving you 80 percent of your results.

That's it! In any given system, 20 percent of what you're doing is responsible for 80 percent of the outcome. So let's look at athletic training. You have one hundred exercises. Twenty of those are going to impact your results by 80 *percent*. Why would you even bother with the other eighty exercises?

If we put this into a time management system, 20 percent of your time is giving 80 percent of your results. Why would you spend that other 80 percent of your time for a return of 20 percent? That's an insanely bad investment of your time and energy.

The whole point of the following exercise is to figure out that supereffective 20 percent, but first we have to figure out your time drains and why you're having them. Each part might feel disjointed but we'll connect them all together in the end.

I can't stress this enough. Take the time to do this. It will change your daily habits and your entire life.

Step Two—What do you want to do?

Now. This is the crux of this whole time-expanding thing:

The biggest reason we give away most of our time is that we're not super clear about what we'd do if we in fact *did have more time.* Oh sure, we have a vague idea that, ya know . . . life would be better if . . .

Time to get specific. This is super important, so do it!

So. *Here!* I've magically handed you three glorious extra hours a day. That's right. Three extra hours to do anything you want with. What would you do with that time?

Seriously. Write this down.

What would you *do*? Dig, *dig,* and be specific.

What would you do with this mystical, elusive extra time?

The more specific you can be, the better.

Remember. You can't make time if you don't know what you're making time for. It's trippy when you think about it. You *know* you need more time, but for what? More laundry? 'Cause, yeah, maybe . . . but really? I don't think so.

If you want more time to spend with your kids, what would you *do with your kids* when you have this time? Play games? Read books? Want to have more time with your spouse? For *what*? Going to dinner? More sex? Write it down.

If you magically had three extra hours, would you write a book? Write an online course? Start a business? Knit? Learn ukulele?

Be specific. Even if it's "sit and be bored." Even if it's "sleep." Brainstorm. Write all the things down. You don't have to curb yourself here. Go for it.

I'll say it again for emphasis. You can't allow for more time if you don't know how you would use that time. Have fun with this!

If I had three extra hours a day I would

_____
_____
_____
_____
_____
_____
_____
_____

Step Three—Big stones first

So you wrote all those things down. All the things you'd do if you did have all this extra time. Was it fun? Frustrating? Were your answers all over the map? Were you almost paralyzed by too many options? As a parent, you may be familiar with this phenomenon. It's nap time, your child goes down, and there's so much to do, you are paralyzed. So you either take a nap or scroll FB 'cause You. Just. Can't. Decide. What. To do.

That's what happens all the time. So you have to figure out what's important _to you._

What should you be focusing on?

We are pulled in so many directions that we can forget our actual priorities. Or maybe we're so busy, we haven't even made something a priority.

This concept is called "big stones first." Imagine you have one big bucket, and you're supposed to fill it with a few big stones, a ton of pebbles, and some sand. You have to fit them all in the finite space of that bucket, and you can't leave anything out. If you put all the sand and pebbles in first, the bucket is going to fill up with all that tiny stuff, and the big stones aren't going to fit. They are going to be stuck on top of all the sand and pebbles, falling out of the bucket.

But if you put the big stones in first, the sand and pebbles will fit in the tiny gaps around the big stones. Everything will fit in your bucket.

In case you're not in the mood for metaphors right now, I'll just say it: the bucket is your time. The big stones are what's important to you. The sand and pebbles are the minutiae of the day that have to get done but aren't a huge priority.

Exercise: What are your big stones?

A few caveats. This is for *you*. Not for society. Not for your friends. *For you and your family.*

Your big stones can change. You have life big stones—big values, big things that are a consistent priority in your life overall. But you also have daily or weekly big stones. Yeah? And those may change over time.

For me, connection with Pascal is a life big stone. Overarching. Always there.

Because we homeschool, social time with friends is a daily big stone. Most days, cleaning the house is sand. Until the mess is out of control, and then it might switch to a big stone for a day. Checking social media is definitely sand.

It's super important to figure out your big stones because

recognizing them will stop you from being influenced by all the *shoulds* society is going to throw at you.

If your big stone is healthy eating, with regular meal planning for your family, that will probably mean you are housebound a bit more than most parents. You'll need to cook and spend more time preparing. It will mean you'll be home more to eat at regular times. *This is totally cool.* Even though society will tell you that keeping your kid busy with constant out-of-the-house activities and that eating out and eating in the car is okay, you have a different big stone.

Likewise, if you're all about adventure and being out in the world all the time, you may have to sacrifice a routine. You may get stuck eating some crappy food out in the world.

The trick? Find your big stones and really, really commit to them, no matter what you see other people on IG or FB doing. It really doesn't matter. Listen to your heart.

What are three life big stones? And what might three weekly big stones be? Three big stones for today?

Pick only three of each. The bucket is only so big. If you pick more than three, you will have too many for your bucket. And that's part of the problem. It's important to remember that stones may shift. You may feel like, OMG, *I have way more than three priorities*. That's why I've made daily, weekly, and life categories. Your life big stones may not play out every day but you need to keep an eye on them. Your daily big stones will shift, as in my above example of cleaning the house. It's not a big thing till the mess gets out of control, right?

Here's a typical example of shifting stones: Seriously limiting your child's screen time is a big stone for you. But now you have a work deadline (a temporary big stone), so your little one gets to crack out on YouTube Kids all afternoon. Your big stone shifted because of life. That doesn't mean it's gone. There's just no room for it in the bucket today.

Daily Big Stones

1._____
2._____
3._____

Weekly Big Stones

1._____
2._____
3._____

Life Big Stones (Don't make these too broad.)

1._____
2._____
3._____

Step Four—Snaking the time drains

Next, we figure out where the time drain is and snake that mofo.

Where *does* all your time go? Now, this is a little tricky 'cause we can start to fool ourselves. I want to assure you I don't give a rat's ass where your time goes. I really don't. This is for you. So be really honest and don't judge it. We need all the puzzle pieces before we put this bad boy together.

Where does your time go?

Here's a tip: Don't count social media. 'Cause, yeah. We all already know we all dick around on social media too much. Clients I work with always brush this exercise off. "Yeah, I already know I waste all my time on Facebook."

Yes, it's a time suck but it's *not the only time suck in your life*. You are losing time other places and I want you to find those places. You get to keep your social media meanderings, I promise.

But right now, go about your day and notice where you are spending huge chunks of time. All of it—the stuff you think is productive, the stuff you judge yourself for, everything in between.

Do not judge anything, and pay attention to all of it.

Do not make a plan to change anything yet.

Just go about your average day. How do you spend your time? You can write it down if you want. Or you can just think about it.

I don't even want to give you examples yet. This is so totally individual.

Three areas of my life I spend a crazy amount of time on

1._____

2._____

3._____

Step Five—Fake productivity

Oh ho! So this one might push your buttons a little bit. That's cool.

So you've looked at your day. What was *glaring*?

We're looking for the *Like, wow!* moments. I sure do check my emails all freaking day!

Or was it texting? Or was it cleaning up after your kids? Folding five loads of laundry? Dusting behind the couch?

Now I need you to take a look at how you spend your day—and find the areas of fake productivity. In our current society, you are praised for productivity. We have absorbed this concept so fully that we often say with pride, "I was so productive today." It feels good to be productive! 'Cause the opposite would be . . . *lazy?* Oooooh, anything but lazy!

We love us some *busy*. We love checking off lists (me, most of all). And I think it's pretty human to want to feel *accomplished*. Which is cool, man.

But let's go back to the 80/20. Only 20 percent of that productivity is producing almost all of your results! Ya know what that means??? Eighty percent is fake. Eighty percent of what you do is *fake productivity*. If 80 percent is producing only 20 percent of what you want, well, it may not be fake but it *is* mindless. It's ineffective.

There is shit that has to get done. Absolutely. No question.

But there's also shit we attend to all throughout the day. When we're bored. Or procrastinating. Or because we're not super clear about what we would do with the time we could free up. We'll talk about fixes in the next step. This step is about finding those areas and being brutally honest with ourselves.

This can be tricky to figure out, so let me give you my personal examples. I found *four* gaping holes that my time was being lost in.

1. Emails. When I looked at my day like I'm asking you to do, I found I was spending a ridiculous amount of time checking/responding to emails.

I run a successful business. I get a ton of email from this. I could check email all day long. I really could. But it doesn't need to be checked all day long. It needs to be checked once a day.

I have to credit Tim Ferriss for changing my view on this. He answers emails *once a week*. And this dude is wicked famous. His autoresponder says, "I answer emails on Friday at four p.m. If this is important and you need to reach me, call me. If you don't have my number, it's not important." OMG . . . *right?*

The reality is we've created an overinflated sense of importance about *everything*.

More important, for me and my time, this is a perfect example of fake productivity. "Look at me . . . I'm working! I'm being productive!" The reality?

- I wasn't super clear about what I wanted to with my spare time.
- In downtime, would-be-bored moments, I would do things like check emails.
- I not only felt (fake) productive, I felt (fake) important. "Oh, I'm so busy. I'm so important. I have to get back to people right away."

Can you see my bullshit there?

2. Facebook for business. I have to use Facebook for business. But, man! The times I would fool myself, getting lost on Facebook for "business." It's totally cool to dick around with Facebook. It is so not cool to fool yourself with fake productivity. If you're gonna dick around, go for it. But don't act like it's work.

3. Texting. I became keenly aware of how often I feel the need to text my friends every thought or every funny thing that happens to me in the day. This is more fake connection than fake productivity. I may feel like I'm connecting with my friends, but the reality is that texting punches a *huge hole* in my time. It creates a need for a back-and-forth. It's also a hotbed of no-tone misunderstandings that have to then be corrected.

I don't consider myself a serial texter, so this one was a bit of a shock to me.

4. Food prep + kitchen cleanup. Holy crap, this one was the big shocker. I was spending a *ridiculous* amount of time in the kitchen. Prepping and cooking food and *cleaning up*. Where's the fake productivity in that? Constantly having a clean kitchen throughout the entire day does nothing for my life. It doesn't bring me closer to those I love, it doesn't make me money, it doesn't bring me lasting joy. I get a fleeting moment of *Oh, how clean my kitchen is!* and that's about it. It was something to do—again, when I wasn't super clear about what it is I wanted more time for.

These are my time drains. I have no idea what yours will be. Yours may be the polar opposite of mine. But all four of those time drains—for me—are things I would do when I had "spare time."

And here's where you have to be brutally honest with yourself.

104

We lose ourselves in fake productivity because a lot of us (myself included) have a trip in our heads about what's productive and what's lazy. Midday, sitting down to read a fiction book, while there are dishes in the sink? What a horrible mother you must be!

Am I right?

And yet dishes *will* be done. But no one, *no one* is going to hand you extra time to read a book. Let alone write a book or learn something new.

We all do this. So if you think you have no areas of fake productivity, you might want to dig a little deeper and be a little more honest with yourself. Bingeing on Netflix instead of going to sleep at a normal time is fake productivity. It feels like me/relax time but it's draining. Staying up too late makes you the least on-your-game the next morning.

So where are your areas of fake productivity? When you have even a small amount of spare time, what do you do that *feels* like you're doing something but *really* you're just messing around?

I am fake productive when I

1._____

2._____

3._____

Step Six—Make a plan

Now it's time to make a plan. This plan is *your* plan, depending on your goals. I'm not about to be all up in here telling you how you should spend your day. If you feel like you would like to pick your nose all day and you never have time to pick your nose, let's reclaim some time for you to pick your nose. In other words, I really don't care *how* you spend your time and *why* you want to reclaim it.

Go back to your exercises. Where did you find yourself using all your time?

Where did you find yourself using fake productivity? There probably was an overlap in those two.

Mine: Like I said, I realized almost all my time drain was happening in the kitchen, with food prep and cleaning. My lifestyle is such that I homeschool and it's only me and Pascal. We both eat when we're hungry. Which means a kind of constant flow of food. And cleaning. BTW, I'm the last living soul without a dishwasher.

Remember, I was also moving toward keeping the kitchen clean as fake productivity.

The fix: I now only do dishes in the morning and evening, when I also do my food prep. All other times, it can wait. Yes, my kitchen is messier. But I have freed up hours. Whatever lunch will be, I make it ahead of time, so it can be grabbed by either of us when we feel like it. The food prep and cleaning happen at the same time while I am in the same room. And I don't multitask. I do those chores together. No phone. No text. Kid, don't bug me. I have literally added hours to my day with this simple shift.

This was *my* shift in this area: 80 percent of my results (dishes done, food cooked) now take 20 percent of my time and energy. If this isn't mind-blowing to you, I think maybe you're not getting it.

When Pascal was little, I read something similar: *Stop picking up toys.*

Pick up toys *once* a day, at the end of the day. Picking up toys all day *feels* like you're doing something. Why not use those spare moments to sit. Relax. Or pick your nose. Whatever.

You may work outside the home, which certainly presents a whole different set of challenges. That makes your time even more precious. I can't possibly try to solve every individual time drain. You're a grown-up. Think creatively and you can find solutions. This is about identifying the problem.

Let's move on to your digital life.

We all have a crazy busy digital life. One of the things that is so hard right now is that we have so many forms of communication. So many ways we can be reached. We can easily get distracted during the day answering FB messages, emails, texts, voice mails. It can be a huge drain on time.

The fix: time chunking. I time chunk all my digital time now.

Email and Facebook: One hour to answer all my emails and *only* once a day. I give myself set times to dick around on Facebook and IG. And I'm strict about keeping that time. I give myself strict times to post for my businesses. Seriously, set a timer for these things. If you don't put a boundary around your time, it will escape out from under you.

Cell phone: I don't keep my phone alerts on. Unless my texting is about making immediate plans, I only check my phone at certain times and answer all the texts at once. Which brings us to: Unless you are expecting someone to call or text for immediate plans that day, *shut off your phone* or keep it in airplane mode. OMG. I can't overstate the magic of airplane mode! It's really that simple. Shut off your phone so you aren't a slave to the dings. Shut off all notifications. Especially if you're trying to make something online. Like writing a book or creating a course or starting an online business. Time chunk your writing.

By time chunking your digital life, I promise you will gain at the very least an hour to your day, if not more. Again, getting 80 percent of your results (communications answered) with 20 percent of your time.

It's worth mentioning as well that constant communication is draining on the soul. Personally, I feel tugged at and pulled apart when I drip out communications all day long. I like to communicate in chunks, get done what needs to be done, and then wallow in real life.

Find your drains and creatively solve them. This will look different for everyone, but the idea is figuring out how you can get 80 percent of the results you need with only 20 percent of your time and energy.

Step Seven—The messed-up, awful culture of busy

I have this new thing I do. When talking with just about anyone, whether I run into them or call them or whatever, I of course say, "How are you?" Nine times out of ten the answer is, "Oh. So busy." My answer now is, "I'm so sorry. Is there anything you can do about that?" I get a pretty stunned response.

Here's your in-your-face, no-holding-back-truth bomb. *You are creating your own state of busy.* And it's ugly, it's serving no one, least of all you (or your family), and you get no bonus points from anyone for being busy. *Stop the culture of busy.* We're stressing ourselves out, diminishing our health and vitality. We are damaging our children and stressing them out. We are on a constant treadmill of busybusybusybusy.

So much of busy is manufactured to keep ourselves from our own thoughts. That's a fact and if you don't like that, take a hard look at it. Yes. We all have to adhere to other people's schedules sometimes. But all the time? I see this *a ton* in parenting. Rushing from activity to activity. Sacrificing connection and downtime for more activities. A huge fear is "But what if they get bored?" And yet we know boredom is the gateway to creativity.

But to hell with the kids for a minute! What about *you*? What about you being bored? Can you even imagine? Let me tell you, it's bliss. It's where great ideas are born. It's where your mind settles into your soul. You can hear your heart beating and telling you its secrets.

We have been indoctrinated with the idea that busy is good. But let's think back to the you-have-three-extra-hours exercise. What would you do with that time? I bet at the bottom of your grand plans was a desire to be still. To lounge. To linger. To read, sleep, relax. You can do that *now*. Every day. You don't even need a vacation. Only you have the power to put down the busy. Don't blame it on activities or the need to do something.

I adore the now-ubiquitous saying, "Create a life you don't need a vacation from." You can do that right now. You can design your life to be any way you want.

I think the worst thing I see out in the world is the idea that you can't control the busy. I see parents all the time *saying* they want more downtime, more snuggles, more quiet days, and those same people sign their kids up for yet another activity. You control this. If you want downtime, you must make room for downtime. Downtime must be a big stone. 'Cause otherwise it won't fit.

Exercises

Actually start thinking (on a regular basis): What's the least I can do? What's the least I *have* to do? This is really hard in our current culture. See what happens in your own head when you say that.

Try wallowing in *lazy*. Play with the word. Try it out. We're so conditioned to think, *What's the* most *I can give?* that giving the *least* feels like cheating. It's not. It's reclaiming your time. And time is the only commodity in the world that you can't get back once it's gone.

We can't loosen up the busy time and make way for boredom and creativity if we have an endless to-do list. If the calendar is always full. If we're constantly running around.

I beg of you. Investigate your own need to be busy. Are you really that busy? Or are you keeping yourself busy to hide, to not live out loud? To not work through your crap? To keep yourself from your own thoughts? To project an image of what you think success looks like?

Bonus: 80/20 Parenting

Oh. This is so good. You can absolutely and totally apply the 80/20 principle to parenting. You might be thinking *What?* I can't give my kid(s) only 20 percent! That's impossible! A good parent gives 110 percent All. The. Time. And, yes, of course the younger your child, the more she actually needs from you. But our generation of parents suffers greatly from two things:

1. **Overparenting.**
2. **Uh-huh parenting.**

I'm sure you're aware of *overparenting*. But maybe not in yourself. We don't have to be there all the time, managing our children. We need to facilitate their growth. We may need to help them negotiate feelings and emotions in relationships. But generally speaking, we could all do with a big dose of leaving them alone a lot more. Of course, when our kids are very young they are needy little suckers and we can't often leave them alone. Is there anything scarier than extended silence with toddlers? Leaving them alone is like a small seed that grows and grows as your child does. I think of it as backing out of parenting slowly, over the years. This means giving them more actual physical space (not hovering over every move they make), letting them make mistakes without rushing in to fix things, finding that magic spot of letting them feel a little frustration without its becoming a meltdown. It's constantly reevaluating: Can she do this by herself? Does he really need my help?

Uh-huh parenting is my term for distracted parenting. Like fake productivity, this is almost fake parenting. We talked about this in the "Connection" chapter. It's looking at your phone or your computer or the book you're reading or just zoning out lost in your own busy thoughts while pretending to pay attention to your kid. You send your kid an *uh-huh* every now and then. To let him know you kinda heard him. To be clear, I'm not telling you to get off your phone. Stay on it. But don't pretend to be engaged with your kid when you're not. Be honest. Tell your child to hang on while you dick around on your phone. *Then* give your little one your full attention. Kids *know* when you're not fully engaged. And guess what? *That makes them needier.* This 20 percent you give—if you *give it fully*—means you can actually back off a large amount of the time.

Listen. We're all trying to create good humans with our

child-rearing. But the principle applies: 20 percent of your efforts are yielding 80 percent of your results. Find that 20 percent so you can ease off your kids. For their sanity. And your time. And the reality? An 80 percent return on raising a good human is a really good chunk.

When it first entered my brain to apply the 80/20 principle to parenting, I was, like, *no way*. Then I realized, Wait . . . this is no different from the empty/full emotion bucket. When we consciously *fill* our kid's emotional buckets, they don't need us as much.

When their buckets are empty, they are needy AF.

I think most families walk around with half a bucket, trying to drip some stuff in as it's being drained. That's where that other 80 percent of your energy goes, right? If you feel like you're giving 100 percent all the time, I'm here to tell you that largely 80 percent of that is pretty ineffective parenting. At a 20 percent yield, it's a terribly poor investment of your time and energy.

Of course, a lot depends on your particular family, your particular kids, the ages of your kids. Parenting isn't a matter of hard-and-fast numbers. But just try this. See where you can back out of ineffective parenting. Uh-huh parenting. Plan to connect with your kids at least once a day. Put the devices away and listen. Look them in the eye. They will get full. Their emotional buckets will be full and you can truly parent from this place.

Maintaining connection seriously takes about 20 percent of your time and energy. And then let them go play. Alone (when applicable). Just keep this perspective in your head as you go about your days and weeks and years. As you watch your child blossom before you.

I work with parents for a living. I see too many parents

draining themselves, bending over backward, striving for 100 percent. Think about it: if 100 percent of you is going to parenting, holy crap! There's nothing left to give! Remember the pebbles and sand taking up all the space and leaving no room for the big stones? This is that.

I will tell you this. I've spent the last year applying this principle. I have actively found and maintained my big stones. I am wallowing in oceans of lazy. My family life, my home, and most important, my connection with Pascal and my connection to my own creativity have been wildly blissful.

I seriously hope you apply all this goodness to your life. Again, I can only give you the concepts; I can't make you apply them. I want you at peace, unfrazzled, de-stressed, fully present in your life with your kids, with your spouse, or with whatever brings you the most joy. No one is going to magically hand you more time. You *must* find it for yourself. You and only you know what's important to you.

The Big Takeaway

Do the exercises in this chapter. I know you probably think you don't have time for this. But if you give this approach a little time and energy, it will change your life in the best ways!

CHAPTER 6

PARENTAL ANXIETY

Never before in the history of time have parents been so anxious about their actual parenting. There are many reasons for this that swirl and collide into a perfect storm. And it can leave you paralyzed. We live in an anxious world. School shootings. Angry internet exchanges. No matter what your political leanings, it's chaotic and feels unstable. Big Brother really does exist, in the form of YouTube. We as parents have to live in mortal fear of screwing up in public and being filmed and going viral.

Over the years, I've noticed a shift that's happened across the parenting landscape. It's subtle but with huge ramifications. There is an expectation that if we just find the magic code, the magic combination of things, we can turn out perfect humans. But *there is no magic code*. And thinking there might be a magic code is what's behind a shit ton of parental anxiety.

There are a few reasons things have gotten so out of whack for us as parents, both in general and particularly with the later toddler years. One I see all the time is this push for early academics doing a lot of damage to our understanding of this age group. In general, we are so focused on those academics that we're leaving out some vital life skills. Life skills that make our little ones feel loved, like they are part of the family and wider community. And make them feel capable. That kind of learning is what builds strong, resilient kids.

Also feeding this particular fire is the Disney-fueled "make childhood magical" frenzy. I got nothing against Disney, mind you. But we're all in a race to make childhood special and magical. You know what makes childhood magical? You don't pay bills! Someone cooks for you! You have all your needs met!

Of course I'm being a bit silly. But also it's true. We focus on making everything special and wonderful and then we're all shocked when we turn out entitled kids who have no emotional fortitude or resilience.

One major contributor is too much input. We're inundated with advice and information thanks to the internet. And it totally shakes our confidence when we have one expert tell us one thing and another tell us the polar opposite.

Social media has given us the illusion that opinion matters and is fact. And you know that saying, "Opinions are like assholes; everyone has one." And, boy howdy, do people have opinions about parenting. It's one of the biggest aspects of my parent coaching: leveling out the "but so-and-so said . . ." I've also been a potty training expert for years and years, and of course that's an area rife with other-mom-know-it-alls. Every single mom I've ever met has been cut to the quick in some online exchange. Having another mom in a random Facebook group tell you in no uncertain terms that you are without a doubt fucking up your child for life is enough to shake even a seasoned parenting pro.

Paralyzed parenting

When Sarah first hired me as a parent coach, we spent at least the first three sessions wading through all the conflicting information she'd been hearing in her mom groups. Her parental anxiety was through the roof! She had zero confidence in her intuition. She couldn't make a single decision without researching the hell out of it. Which led to more anxiety because no mom in the history of the world has time to research the hell out of every decision she makes without sacrificing a whole lot of time. And that very research can lead you down rabbit holes of doom.

We actually have too much information available to us. And what's worse is we have too many outlets for others to share their opinions about all that information. And what's happened is we've lost our gut feelings, our intuition along the way. We have a gut instinct about what to do about a situation with our kids, and then massive doubt creeps in.

No matter what you choose to do, how you choose to parent, you can find some "expert" who tells you this will result in raising a sociopath. And another "expert" who says this is the one and only thing to do.

This is what's making us anxious.

This is what's contributing to what I call *paralyzed parenting*. I coined this term a long time ago. We have so much conflicting information at our fingertips that often I see parents so undecided, they become paralyzed and do nothing. This happens all the time in potty training. Child-led versus parent-led approaches create such indecision that parents often just put off potty training until it becomes more difficult and they're up against school requirements. They tell me honestly, "I was so busy researching and trying to determine the right way of doing things that time got away from me."

Life moves on every single day. If we are lost in researching the best way to do any part of parenting, our kids will be grown before we can even implement anything.

What's really heartbreaking, though, is how all this information undermines our intuition. I say this in my potty training book and I'll say it here ad nauseam: you are the expert on your child. I am an expert at certain things because I've worked on them a long time. I have a million tips and tricks to help. But I will never know your child like you do. Ever. I will never live in your shoes.

In vaginal childbirth, there's a phase called *transition*. This is the baby making her way out of the birth canal. Widely recognized as the hardest part of vaginal birth, transition is the dark pain cave for mothers. This is the moment when your support team becomes useless. It doesn't matter who is helping you breathe or bringing you ice chips. You and you alone are the one who's going to push this human out of your vagina. It's a place where most women go way inward and become silent and go to work.

Parenting is like that. For both men and women. There comes a moment when you have to let all the information go, look that particular child in his eyes, and check your gut on what to do. I promise you there's a really good chance you're right.

My goal is always to bring parents back to their intuition. All the experts in the world are useless if your anxiety is overriding your intuition. The very best thing you can do for your child is go into that cave. Go inward. Find *your* bond with your child. Look at the child you have, not the child you want. Parenting philosophies are the number one killer of good parenting.

When you step out of your ideas about parenting, you can see the child you have. For example, I work with many parents who say something along the lines of "I know she needs routine. I think she really needs a strict routine. But that's not really my style. I'm way looser and it doesn't suit me." Well, you don't get that option. We all really, really need to parent the child we have.

Brené Brown calls this "minding the gap." It's the difference between who you want to be as a person—and who you want your child to be—and who you both are now. The vision you have versus what's happening now. Let's go back to Jim and Maya and their overscheduling having the opposite effect from what they wanted. They envisioned slower days and yet kept creating chaotic ones, and they fell right into that gap. Many parents ask the question "Why can't he just be a quiet kid?" That's a useless question that creates anxiety. *He's not.* Be cautious not to step into that gap.

It's not all about you

Another huge source of anxiety is our attaching ourselves to our children's accomplishments and failures as part of our identity. I know you're a long way off from this but at some point you'll be privy to parental conversations about SATs and college admissions. Holy crap. You listen to these parents and you'd think *they* were the ones who took the test. For some people, their entire identity revolves around their kid's accomplishments. The flip side of this is a crazy-making need to make sure your child never fails.

Have you ever felt the scathing look of judgy moms because your kid is the one eating sand in the sandbox? Or your kid is hitting, not sharing, or whatever. You know what I'm talking about. And you feel a rush of shame? We have to disconnect from that shame. Kids do stupid things. Kids act like jerks. Kids make massive mistakes. That doesn't mean we've failed as parents. It's not always about you. If you can release a little bit of that feeling—that you are responsible for everything your child does—you will have gone a long way toward easing your anxiety.

You should also remember that the world has a lot invested in your feeling not confident. Entire markets and industries depend on it. Clicks online convert to money or in many cases data, which is second-best to cash these days. Big diaper companies are highly invested in your feeling not confident about potty training. Hell, in one generation, they've extended their product's life span by *two years*! Keeping parents mucked up and insecure sells things. Even if it's just opinions.

In most areas of this book, I give you free range with social media. I know it's a part of most of our lives and I try to give you helpful tools for managing it. But if you find you are anxious about your parenting, the best thing you can do is stay off the internet. There's just too much information, and it won't help you in any way. Same goes for research. For horror stories. For medical advice. We all do a quick google about things to do with our kids. But if you end up going down rabbit holes that feed your anxiety, just stay off the internet.

I once worked with a mom who was literally giving herself an ulcer over environmental concerns. The chemicals in the air, in her home, on her shoes, in the water. Yes, we all should be informed, but there's something to be said for staying sane as well. There's also the simple fact that if you're going nuts thinking of all the things that could potentially go wrong, all the ways your little one could get hurt, you simply aren't being present with your child in the moment. And that's really the best thing you can do for your child.

In a fairly benign example, I'm sure you've seen the parent obsessed with keeping a child clean at the playground. "No, no.

Don't do that. You'll get dirty." After a while, you start think-ing, OMG, *leave that kid alone.* You can replace *dirty* with *hurt.* "No, no, you'll get hurt. Don't do that. Don't. Don't. Don't." Sure, a lot of parenting is saying "no" and "don't" and keep-ing boundaries. But that parent in the park? That's not really parenting. That's limiting the child and there's no connection there. There are only blockades and walls. That child is going to kick back soon and *hard.* Or that child isn't going to be able to make a move without approval. Neither result is good.

Kicking parental anxiety

So what can you do if you find yourself riding a high-anxiety train? First off, recognize it. Do you find yourself winding up? Listen to your voice. Is it often squeaky or high-pitched? Do you feel shame in your body (often this feels like physical heat in the body)? Do you feel like you need to fix something in your parenting right now? Do you find yourself feeling panicky or jittery, always unsure about the next step? Do you leap to catastrophic thinking? I work with parents who literally have anxiety about college admission and their child is three. That's a version of catastrophic thinking. A more severe version is thinking your child is in imminent danger all the time.

Here are some things you can do to calm your fears:

- Breathe. I know that can sound stupid, but take a few full breaths. Ground yourself in the present.
- List three great things right now. In the present.
- Connect with your child asap. Get right down on the floor with her.

- Look her in the eyes. Ask her a question. Feel the grip on your heart loosening. Stay off-line. No amount of research or social media will be calming.
- Learn a quick meditation that you can do in a few minutes. There are thousands you can look up. Use your internet powers for good.
- Gather a safe village. Be open with a few good friends. "You guys, sometimes I start to panic that I'm totally fucking this up." Trust what they have to say. Anxiety can tell us stupid stories and you may have to rely on a trusted outside source until you find your intuition again.
- *Listen.* Listen to your gut and don't be quick to dismiss it. Honor it. It's like a muscle: the more you use it, the stronger it becomes.

With anxiety as with just about anything, there's a range of normal. Most levels of anxiety don't interrupt our lives, don't often keep us up at night, and can be "talked down" with reason and logic. If you're experiencing anxiety that you really can't control, that's interrupting your life and/or relationships or affecting your connection with your child, it's always good to seek help. In a report published in the *Harvard Review of Psychiatry*, researchers found that in women who were not receiving clinical treatment, 30 percent of women with postpartum depression were still depressed up to three years after giving birth. Postpartum depression can also look like anxiety and excessive worry. All the feelings I've discussed here are within a normal range of parental anxiety. My goal is to bring your attention to your anxiety so you can lean into your intuition more. The bond with your child comes with that intuition built in. Learn to trust it. Back off of everyone else's opinion and lean into the connection with your child. You'll know the answers.

A large part of parental anxiety is future tripping. "I better do the right thing or she'll end up being (some version of not perfect)." There's a great quote floating around: "There's no such thing as being a perfect parent. So be a real one." To me, being a "real" one means all the things we've been talking about. Real connection. Doing gut checks with yourself instead of jumping to the internet for advice. Really seeing your child as he is, not as you'd like him to be. Creating a safe tribe of like-minded parents who aren't all judgy.

And feeling confident in the job you're doing. This often means going against the grain of society, or rather the current parenting trends. A lot of what's in the kid section of this book is going against that grain. Building your confidence will take practice but it's worth it.

The Big Takeaway

You are shaping the child you are raising, but you are not creating this human. You cannot create the perfect child who then grows into the perfect adult. There is no magic code that will make that happen. Most parental anxiety comes from the idea that you are somehow messing up. Sink into love and connection first and foremost, and you really can't go wrong.

CHAPTER 7

REACTIONARY PARENTING

We all act and react: this is human interaction. Often parents come to me because they feel like they aren't reacting "properly" to situations with their child or that their reactions have gotten out of control, even if just for a moment.

I often hear the phrase "I don't know why this bugs me so much." Even apart from parenting, I find it fascinating why some things bug some people. Just a simple scroll through Facebook and you can find someone going crazy over something that just wouldn't bug you at all. Or your spouse gets super irritated by something the kids do and you're like, "Really? Honey. Chill. They're just being kids." And vice versa, of course.

We all react differently because each one of us sees the world through our own lens. We all have our own filter, which is built on our experiences from day one. We build this unique filter without any thought through every interaction and experience we've had from the moment we were born. You may already be sick of me saying that our children are constantly learning. They don't do what we say, they do what we do. They learn their behaviors through and from us and how we react. Well, check it out. You were once a child and that happened to *you* as well.

Most of us don't spend a whole lot of time thinking about how we learned to be who we are, unless we've had a huge, obvious problem or trauma. Just like our eyes may filter light differently or our ears may perceive sounds differently, everybody's hearts and minds filter information differently. And, I'd venture to say, the differences are on a much larger scale. They even spill over into our huge political divisions, right? I mean *how could anyone* like that other guy? When we feel it's so freaking obvious that the person we're behind is clearly better?

It's our filters. The emotional and intellectual filters that each one of has formed out of our unique experiences. Then our children come along, and they are our hearts walking around outside our bodies. We are flooded with societal and media messaging about what makes a perfect parent. We are on constant display thanks to cell phone video cameras and YouTube. We are also people with tender spots that directly correlate to our experiences.

When we find ourselves reacting strongly to our children, we must go inward. Yes. Three-, four-, and five-year-olds certainly bring on some challenging behavior. In the end, though, very few kids display life-threatening behaviors (though certainly that can happen in extreme cases). Which means our reactions have been triggered by something inside us.

In my experience, I've found it's one of two things. One, a childhood wound that hasn't been worked through and healed. Or two, a core value that has been shaken.

Childhood wounds

We all have them. For some people, these wounds could be huge and based in major trauma. What I have found, though, is that people who've had big trauma, myself included, tend to know they have these big, gaping wounds and then tend to get help to heal and work through them.

There are, however, many smaller wounds that affect all of us. We all had an experience of feeling deep shame as a child. Maybe a teacher humiliated you in front of the whole class. Maybe a bully taunted you on the bus. Your parents shut down your feelings. Teeny tiny shames, but nonetheless, very deep. Very few of us can look back on how we were parented and say we felt it was perfect. Which is completely normal, because no human is perfect.

But if you don't acknowledge and heal those wounds (usually through some form of therapy), they will affect your parenting in one of two ways: one, your reactions (and overreactions) to your child; and two, what I call *oppositional parenting*. I see both consistently in my work. How we were raised, where our childhood wounds are, these things affect us and we must start peeling away our parental onion layers. Because guess what? If you have an unhealed childhood wound, I can guarantee your child is here to put salt in it to make sure you pay attention. This creates reactions that can be intense in us.

Oppositional parenting is blindly parenting only in opposition to how we were parented. We've covered this idea a bit in chapter 1, but there's also oppositional parenting because of wounds. Let's say your mom was a type A control freak who was very authoritarian. You never got to have a say; your feelings and preferences never counted. You then have a child and swear you will never do that. So you go to the polar opposite and are wildly permissive.

When I started working with Isa, she was struggling because her daughter Clara was a "hot mess" (her words, not mine). Her behavior was all over the map, and Isa was starting to suspect that she might need testing to see if Clara had some sort of diagnosis. There's normal whackadoodle toddler behavior and then there's behavior verging on what almost looks psychotic.

At a first, surface glance, it did almost seem like there could be something wrong with Clara's brain chemistry. She was up and down emotionally; she had violent mood swings and frequent and extended tantrums. Isa was becoming afraid of her and almost never wanted to take her out of the house.

I had Isa walk me through a typical few days, asking her to be really specific about the particular things she said and did, particularly as they precipitated a "Clara event." As we dug a little deeper, I started to pick up on a theme in Isa's behavior. She had almost no boundaries, she gave far too many open choices to Clara, and there was no follow-up even when she did try to hold a boundary. When I'm working with a family, we do a lot of talking, digging, and question asking. Sometimes the underlying issue isn't apparent. With Isa, I started to realize how often our conversations were peppered with something along the lines of "My mother was awful. She never let me have any choices."

Bingo. Isa was not parenting for her and Clara, in the here and now. Isa was parenting to undo some damage in *her* relationship to *her* mother. See how that works? Of course she was doing what she thought was best! And don't misunderstand me, Isa was a devoted mom working hard to make her parenting better. However, the end result was unconscious parenting in a way that was only in opposition to how she herself was parented. Clara was not being taught how to navigate the world. She was being sort of thrown into it to make her own way. Now, let me be clear here so you can see the difference. Isa was a *wildly* attentive mom. But emotionally, she wasn't giving Clara the rules. And Clara was as a result literally going bonkers.

The other part of the equation is our reactions to our children. In Isa's case, besides not setting boundaries, she also wasn't reacting authentically to Clara's behavior. Her parents had been strict disciplinarians who punished her pretty severely for even minor infractions. She'd vowed that she would never do that to Clara. And, yes! We definitely can take helpful cues from things we hated about our parents. If we were shamed and strictly punished for small things, it is absolutely good and right that we are aware of breaking that cycle with our own kids. But Isa was doing it blindly. She was just never, ever going to reprimand Clara at all.

Again, this left Clara careening wildly through her little life. As I'll continue to say over and over again, these are the years of learning. If we don't teach our kids the rules of the road when they're toddlers, they are bound to drive like little maniacs.

Isa was creating a different problem than her parents had with her, though not as different as you might think. Clara was emotionally unsafe. Stop for a minute, because this is so intriguing. Just like Molly and David in the "Boundaries" chapter, Isa was literally creating the *same emotional environment* that she was actively trying to avoid. Its flavor was slightly different, but she was putting Clara on psychologically shifting territory. Without *any* boundaries. Letting Clara decide everything. Clara may not have been feeling the same sense of shame that Isa had growing up. But by not reacting to wonky behavior, Isa wasn't giving Clara any rules at all. Isa grew up being micromanaged with discipline. Clara was growing up with no guidelines whatsoever.

Our work together shifted to comparing Isa's oppositional parenting to parenting in the moment. We had to work through the idea that being firm is not being mean. That reprimands are necessary so children can learn right from wrong. Occasionally, a small consequence may be in order. We especially worked hard on Isa's not giving Clara endless choices. In fact, it really only took working a bit through Isa's childhood sludge for her to be able to make a few tweaks in her parenting.

It was a relatively quick fix, believe it or not. Once Isa wasn't swinging the pendulum so far away from her parents' parenting, she was able to arrive at peaceful parenting with rules and boundaries. Clara responded typically: she pushed back. When you suddenly set boundaries that you've never set before, please expect your child to push up against them. *She has to.* To see if they're real, if you are serious, if you do in fact mean business. Children have to push up against you *to feel safe*! It's such a strange paradox because it feels like the opposite. It can feel like they are saying, "*No!* I don't want this rule. I don't want this boundary." But what they are really saying, if we could articulate the emotional response, is, "Thank God you're telling me where to stop. But I have to make sure. I have to test you. Because if you don't hold the boundary, I'll have to push more." I know that sounds weird, but it's true.

Own your own triggers

How we react to our children is often based in our own crap. It just really is. Anything that makes you blow a gasket is usually a trigger point. And it doesn't always have to be based in an old wound. We all have a gaping blind spot called What If I'm a Shitty Parent? And it makes us lose our minds at times. Having worked with thousands of potty training clients, I can tell you this issue is often prominent in potty training. Parents go *nuts* if potty training isn't going well. Why? Because, most often, deep in them somewhere is What If I'm a Shitty Parent? What If I Am Fucking This Up? And as with all trigger points, our conscious and unconscious mind will work overtime at avoiding such a painful notion.

Take some time to sit with yourself. What behaviors drive you bonkers? What does your child do that takes you to the very edge? Explore within that a bit. There's always going to be bad behavior that needs to be adjusted. *Always*. For the rest of your parenting career. We distinguish these normal conflicts from reactionary parenting by how heated we feel in the moment.

Most kid behavior is what I call "in normal range." They are blossoming into people with big personalities. That means trying on jerk behavior. That means testing limits. And sometimes it means being kids, acting like they have no responsibility—because they don't. Acting like they have no judgment—because they don't. Yet. As I've said, I'm sure you've been out in the world with friends or even seen it happen with strangers: a parent goes over the edge about something and you think, "Jeez, that wasn't *that* bad." You don't have a trigger point for the behavior you witnessed. That other parent sure does. And we all have our blind spots.

The thing to remember is that when you find yourself getting your knickers in a bigger bunch than usual, it's usually because of a trigger point. If this concept is brand-new for you, I highly suggest checking out Dr. Shefali Tsabary. She has some amazing content on YouTube and Ted Talks.

Core values

Now, there is a second cause for reactionary parenting. It's your child pushing up against your value system. When I say value system, I'm talking about a very specific concept that lies deep within you. We all have core values that drive us and our behavior. These core values shape who we are as people. If you ever have found yourself saying something along the lines of "Well, I'm just not that kind of person," you are speaking about your core values.

If I was to ask you right now what your values are, you would probably say something like "Family, education, being a good parent." While those are awesome answers, they are far too vague.

When you get more specific about your values, you can begin to see how they really do shape who you are as a person and who you are as a parent. One thing I consistently see in my work with families is that very often parents have a core value that they are unaware of. Let me give an example I see quite frequently. *Respect.* A lot of parents shy away from the notion of respect because enforcing respect in a toddler can sometimes come off as very authoritarian.

You would definitely have to be in that "governing" zone. Yet, if you're a parent who's done a lot of reading and online searching, you may have crafted a parenting philosophy that goes against such enforcement. Or you may make the classic mistake of trying to logic your toddler into respect. Logic at this age is futile; repetition and consistency are the winners for toddlers.

Another potential pitfall with the notion of respect is that it can seem like it's totally obvious.

When a family comes to me because their toddler is just flat-out sassing them, we do our usual talking out of typical days. I will give them a list of values and ask them to pick three. They usually pick some combination like generosity, humor, and compromise. I ask the question "So then why does this sassing behavior bother you?" Most often parents are flabbergasted. The answer seems *so obvious* to them that they can't believe I've missed it.

The conversation goes something like this:

Me: Why does this behavior bother you?

Them: Well, because it's wrong.

Me: Why is it wrong?

Them: Because I don't like it. It's rude.

Me: Why is it rude?

Them: Because it's disrespectful.

Me: Why is disrespectful bad?

Them: (*getting very aggravated*) Because you have to be respectful to your parents.

Me: Why does he have to learn that?

Them: Because I want him to learn to be respectful to other people.

Me: So, what I'm hearing is that respect is very important to you. Probably we could say it's a major core value.

Them: Everyone should be respectful.

Me: No. That's not a value for some families. Some families value creativity over respect. It's important to *you*, so it's a guidepost for you. You picked humor as a core value. You could potentially see this behavior as humorous.

As you can see, they initially didn't pick respect as a core value; it didn't seem to factor into their parenting at first. But it turns out, respect is very important to them. The reality is that if respect is important to you, you will have to govern more than your initial philosophy may account for. When you look at your core values and your parenting values, it's very easy to turn on a lofty notion. It's very easy to think of how you'd like your parenting to *look* or how you'd like it displayed. Yes. Our parenting is often on display, or we put it on display on purpose (on social media, in public). This means we're not just parenting but also worrying/thinking about what our parenting looks like to others. Which then puts us in a position of not being authentic. We may pepper our IG feed with *some* of the rough stuff, but I've never seen anyone post something like "Rough day trying to figure out what makes my parenting self tick and learned that I need to enforce respect because that's really important to me on a core level." We just don't do that. It's just something for us to be aware of in our parenting inner world.

Most people's first pick of values are fake-outs. We all will tend to pick things we'd *like* to be true. Or that sound good. But if a value is not actually one of the most important to us, it's not the value that we're attempting to parent with.

Just like with trigger points, figuring out where your values are being shaken or pushed against is fairly easy to see once you get in the habit. It really is anything that makes you blow a gasket. Here's the other tricky thing to remember: our core values tend to be so obvious to us that we often overlook them because they seem to be a universal life rule, one that *everyone* should be following.

I once worked with an amazing family. The mom was a visual artist, the dad was a professional snowboarder. They valued creativity and individuality head and shoulders above any other value. They really didn't give a rat's ass about respect. In fact, their kids probably looked pretty rude to most people. It was unimportant to them. Their values were creativity, nonconformity, and courage. And you can tell me all you want, "Well. Children should show respect!" but you have to understand: that is important to *you*. I'm with you on respect. It's actually really important to me as well. However, you have to recognize that it's not for everyone. This becomes important as you figure out your core values because many people gloss over something like respect, thinking it's a given. It's not.

Things get further mucked up when two parents have opposing core values. These differences may have been fun in the beginning before you had kids. However, when you bring them into your parenting, you and your partner may find yourselves extremely at odds. What if Mom says, "This behavior needs to stop right now!" and Dad says, "Eh. What's the big deal?" Right then and there, you know you guys don't have the same parenting values.

Take the time to look the table on the next page. Take some time with your partner. Go through and be really honest about your individual core values and then your parenting core values. This is a wonderful opportunity to do some conscious parenting and to really see and acknowledge your partner and the family. It's also a fantastic feeling when we the parents are fully in control of our emotions. It's bound to happen that we lose it occasionally, but I find that most parents love understanding why it happens. Understanding gives you an edge. If you know why you're having a meltdown, you can catch it faster the next time and keep working on it.

Exercise

This exercise was formulated in my work with Samantha Kettle, PsyD, and Eric Mayhew, LSW.

Here's the deal with values. We all come with our own personal ones, as do our partners. When you first started dating, you may have been drawn to someone with similar values as you, consciously or unconsciously. You may have also been drawn to someone who balances your values. How many times do we say that our better half balances us? A lot. She's the calm to my crazy. He levels me out.

In almost all cases, though, we date, we go out, we have

fun. We don't sit around and talk about our values. Maybe we do but in a lofty, vague way, not in the specific way that I'm suggesting for this exercise. You might think, "Wow, he'll be a great dad." Or "I love that she values higher education so much. That means a lot to me."

Then there's a relationship and getting married. Again, we don't sit around talking about this stuff. There's a wedding to plan and pay for. It's all very exciting. Then there's a house or travel and being married. And then you get pregnant. Oh! And there's dreaming and planning, but very few people anticipate the actual daily grit of parenting. You may decide on how you'll split the night feedings. Or the endless diaper changing. If one person will stay home and the other will work. But I'm betting a whole lot of money that you don't anticipate the crazy toddler years. You can't. There's no way for you to know the shit you will be dealing with.

Yeah, you may decide together that there is *no way* there will be stickers on your car window. You may decide that you *will absolutely* keep going out to fine-dining restaurants because you *will* be in full control over your child at all times. I seriously hope you're laughing as hard as I am right now writing this. I love remembering the type of parent I knew I would be before actually becoming one. It's like one of my favorite things to think about. And die laughing.

My point is you don't think of the small, nagging crap that comes up in everyday parenting. You usually don't take your two sets of personal values and meld them into a Venn diagram to discover your family values. If you find that you feel unsupported by your partner in any area of parenting, it's usually because of this: you find something terribly important that your partner does not. It happens to all of us.

So let's take a minute to do this exercise to get a rough

idea of where your values truly lie. This doesn't have to be, nor should it be, drudge work. Keep it fun and light and in the spirit of exploration and discovery.

Here's an example of a few values that are specific. You are welcome to come up with your own, but stay away from anything super vague. "To be a good dad" is far too vague. It gives you no actual direction in your daily parenting. If your kid throws his milk across the room, "to be a good dad" isn't going to help you.

Values

Acceptance	Honesty
Adventure	Humor
Art	Inner Peace
Authority	Integrity
Autonomy	Intelligence
Beauty	Knowledge
Belonging	Mastery
Challenge	Mindfulness
Compassion	Music
Compromise	Nonconformity
Courage	Order
Creativity	Passion
Curiosity	Practicality
Dependability	Respect
Family	Risk
Fitness	Routine
Freedom	Stability
Generosity	Tradition
Gratitude	Wealth

We all have personal values and we all have family values. You may not care personally about wealth, but making sure your family is well set up financially may be a family value.

Sit with your partner/spouse and each pick three personal values but don't share them with each other right away. Pick only three, because you need to prioritize. Think of this collection as a garden that you are tending and cultivating. You can't plant everything you want, or the garden will get choked and none of the plants will thrive. Your garden can change. You aren't picking these values for the rest of your life, just for this phase.

For couples experiencing rocky times in their marriage, this exercise can be supremely helpful. What you valued as a single person entering a relationship has probably drastically changed over the course of coming together and having a family. It's especially worth noting if you feel like all of sudden you don't know your partner anymore. Things change and it's important to acknowledge where and when they do.

Now, again individually, pick your three family values. These are the things that are important to you as a family. Remember: take the time to really tune into yourself. Think of what's really important to you right now. There are no right or wrong answers. When you're done, share them with each other. Get a Venn diagram going on for where you meet, where you don't. Individual values may cause trigger points in your parenting. Family values should most certainly put you and your partner on the same page. This exercise shouldn't be confrontational. It should give you a huge springboard for conversation. If you value routine and your partner values adventure, you will be at odds. You may get super pissed if a half hour before bedtime, she wants to take the kids for a starry night drive to get ice cream. You may be like *"What the hell? The kids have to be in bed in a half hour!"* And she may be like *"OMG! Loosen up! It's an adventure."*

So then there might have to be finessing. Maybe an agreement that the toddler years are for routine and then mad adventure awaits for the next stage of childhood. Maybe it's that weekends are for adventure, weekdays are for routine.

This exercise will most assuredly help with parenting as a team, but what happens when your kid presses against a value? Suppose your child is a back talker and tries to negotiate her way out of everything. If you value respect, you're likely going to blow a fuse. You might have a knee-jerk reaction that says, "You shouldn't talk to me like that." But if you value autonomy or creativity or freedom, you might see that you have a little lawyer on your hands. You might see value in her behavior. Then you might take a minute and say, "You know, I can see your brain working really hard to find a different solution. I appreciate that about you and we can talk about it, but for now we really have to leave the house." Knowing what's important to you at this phase will guide you as to how you should respond in the moment.

Remember the notion of "minding the gap." If your child does or says something that triggers you, it's because his behavior is falling through the gap between what's happening now and your vision of what you'd like to see happen.

The values exercise is really about you. What's important to you? What's driving your particular train? Your answers will help guide you and your partner when you get a little lost in parenting, as we all do. You can revisit these values whenever you feel a shift happening. And remember, heading into year three with your child will most definitely create a seismic shift. If you and your partner are not on the same page, revisit this list. Be calm and curious and come to some common ground. Because there's always common ground. It takes communication and honesty to find it.

The Big Takeaway

With very minor exceptions, our little kids' behavior should not elicit a crazy reaction from us. Without a doubt, it's our stuff. I've given you a few tools here for now, but I hope you take on examining your values as a lifelong adventure. Learning about yourself and what you value and what makes you lose it—these are crazy good lessons for every human. It's not enough to say, "They're wrong." In some alternative universe they're not wrong. It's not enough to say, "That's just the way it is." Nothing is written in stone. You can't continually say, "Well, this is how I am." Learn why. Learn what's underneath.

THE KID PART
OF THE BOOK

In any relationship, it takes two to tango. We just looked at ourselves and the work we need to do as parents. That work often takes awareness and self-reflection. Hopefully, you learned how your inner process affects your outer actions and reactions. This section is the flip side: our kids. The whole crux of my work is that any behavior is the symptom of something going on inside. Too often, we try to put a Band-Aid on the behavior without looking at the *why*. What is going on inside your child that is bringing about this behavior?

A few hugely important things to bear in mind, always:

Most "bad behavior" is caused by

- acting out of feelings.
- testing your boundaries and their limits.
- curiosity: your child thinking, "What happens if I do this?"
- your child not being appropriately challenged and therefore becoming challenging.

Bored. Not bad.

What I'm finding almost across the board is that we are going above our kids' developmental limits in some areas and not challenging them nearly enough in other areas.

I'll never forget the frantic email I received from a strung-out mama named Sarah.

"I need your parent coaching. I can't take it anymore! My three-year-old son went into the fridge and pulled out a pan of red Jell-O. *That wasn't set yet.* I have a kitchen soaked in red Jell-O liquid! He's so bad lately! He gets into everything and it's like he's intent on destroying things!"

We booked a session immediately. Sarah could have vented for hours. This little dude was running her ragged. Anyone looking in might think this kid was on a tear. But no! In reality, the first thing I told her was, "He's not *bad*. His behavior is not *bad*. He's terribly *curious*! He's looking for stimulation, which looks like looking for trouble."

His name was Jason and he had just turned three. And his little brother David was ten months old. And Mom was pretty sure they would be going for a third child. So she did what most parents do: she kept all the toys and stuff and things from Jason to pass on to David and potentially another child.

The problem was that she never really leveled up Jason's environment. At three years old, he was still surrounded by toys and games that weren't meeting his new challenge-craving brain. His puzzles were still the wooden Melissa & Doug ones with a single piece that fits into a single hole. Easy! He had mastered memory games. Blocks? They're okay, but hmm . . .

what happens if I start to throw them? Or put them in the toilet? Oh! Now that sounds fun!

Let's see what happens. . . .

This is what Jason was up to. He wasn't necessarily trying to bug the hell out of Sarah. He was in full-blown challenge and curiosity mode. His brain was developing at a rapid rate and he just couldn't contain trying to figure out all the wonders of this world.

He was bored, not bad.

When a kid isn't being challenged developmentally, he's going to go looking for a challenge. Does your little one seem hell-bent on finding trouble? Bugging siblings? Butting heads with you? Chances are this kid is looking for a challenge, not trouble.

"What happens if I . . ." can, yes, be limit testing. But it can also be real curiosity. Let's take a second here to be clear about limit testing. It's a parenting buzz term that can be confusing. Your job as the parent is to set the rules and boundaries. Your child's developmental job is to push against those limits. Limit testing is twofold: children test those limits/boundaries you've set to make sure you mean it. But they also test their own limits to find out what they are capable of and "what happens if I do this . . ."

Your average three-year-old is wildly different from just a year ago. With individuation, he is fumbling to find out how he is separate from you. He is entering deep play, which often looks like not listening. He is gaining mastery over his physical abilities and really needs to test the limits of what his little body can do. He doesn't want to be a baby anymore but he still needs a lot of help. He doesn't want to be told what to do, yet he still needs direction.

There's just so much happening.

The entire focus of this kid section is all the things we can do to help you "level up" to meet these challenges. But also to point out the way we are collectively stymieing some of this growth, which is frustrating for the child and a large reason you may be getting so much shitty behavior. We're looking to really foster your child's amazing developmental growth.

Everything at this age is inherently "educational." Oh my, our society loves the word "educational." This age is nothing *but* learning. I want to show you how to challenge your child in a way that matches up with what's happening developmentally. We want to get back to vital play that builds a solid foundation for the academic work that comes later on.

This is the kind of play that builds confidence, risk assessment, core muscles, and whole body awareness.

We'll talk about how to blend all kinds of risk, challenges, and muscle building. And how letting your child just play and keeping up with their busy minds will ease up on the drama you may be experiencing. Let me put your mind at ease: you don't need something formal and structured for your child to be learning. There are many, many ways we can help build patience, empathy, and critical thinking without having to actively and obviously teach these.

We'll work in three main areas:

- Engaging the mind
- Working with the body
- Understanding the behavior

A couple of side notes and resources before we jump in.

Bad child versus bad behavior. It's important to distinguish "you're so bad" from "your behavior is very bad right now." When you call a child bad, psychologically this can be interpreted as the child himself is bad, which can lead to a core belief that will damage the child. We say "bad behavior" because the child isn't bad but, yes, her behavior in the moment can certainly be very crapalicious.

I've found the following to be excellent other resources on these vast topics of risk-taking, physicality, and learning versus education.

- Dr. Peter Gray writes consistently for *Psychology Today*. I find his work fascinating. His main shtick is self-directed education: homeschooling, unschooling, and free learning. However, there's much in his work that can be applied to your own home even if you have no desire to jump into any kind of formal homeschooling. The reality is, we all homeschool even if it's part time and our kids go to a formal pre- or elementary school. Few of us pick our kids up from school and then don't do anything with them. Dr. Gray's research into the history of play and how humans learn is constantly stretching my thinking.
- *The Land* is a documentary about junkyard playgrounds, a movement that began in Wales and is gaining ground. These playgrounds literally look like junkyards and are rife with potentially unsafe things, like rusty nails, broken

boards, and a fire pit. But watching children manage risk with other kids is mind-blowing.

- *50 Dangerous Things (You Should Let Your Children Do)* is now a book but started as a ten-minute TED Talk. I highly recommend the TED Talk as a jumping-off point. Keeping our kids in a bubble of safety is not part of healthy development. Your little crazy one might need some more old-school risk-taking. You'll find she'll develop critical thinking, executive functioning skills, and excellent risk assessment if you ease up on the "Be careful!"

CHAPTER 8

STOP EDUCATING

Okay. I know this is a slightly inflammatory chapter title, but bear with me. Except for maybe Finland, the world has gone flipping crazy with education. I am vehemently against the early rush on academics. It's causing our kids stress, it's developmentally inappropriate, it's the source of much drama and many behavioral issues, and most of all it breaks our connection with our kids.

There is a huge difference between education and learning. Let's be clear: children, in fact all humans, are constantly learning. Formal education is academics: it's structured, based in curriculum, and largely pushed along by the notion that we can fill a person with necessary information. It is often passive; the person receiving the information has not asked for that particular information.

Learning is active, it's curious, and it's intrinsic. We are all learning all the time. If you've ever utilized that new fan-fangled thing called Google, you are learning. You got curious about something, you took action, and in most cases, you did it for you, not for a gold star, not for a degree. You did it because you wanted to know.

The push for early academics is putting too much emphasis

on education and leaving so much learning behind. Kids in kindergarten are being asked to sit all day, and they are expected to be reading fluently by the end of the year. Kids as young as three are being asked to write letters with little hands that haven't developed the proper muscles. Occupational therapists and educators are pleading for change, as most of this rush on academics is being pushed along by new standards.

The push is also causing parents a tremendous amount of stress. I have worked with families who can't find time to potty train because of their three-year-old's academic and extracurricular activities. Three-years-olds with math tutors. This is real. Parents are already panicking about getting into the right college when their child is three years old.

If you know my potty training work, you know I preach against "future tripping." It's really hard to stay present and connected to the child in front of you if you're concerned about that child fourteen years in the future.

Childhood is not a race. And yet many of us want to get a jump on early academics. There is a tremendous fear that our kids won't stay ahead of the curve.

But we're missing a whole lot in there. In the example of one potty training family, I had to gently ask the parents, "Could she miss her math tutor to learn how to use the toilet? That seems like a more valuable skill at this age." The parents were good-natured and were able to laugh at their eagerness for education over a pretty important life skill.

Preschoolers are *crazy* good learners. You know how active and curious they are. They are clamoring for autonomy and independence. Instead of fostering those skills, we consistently think we need to fill them with education. At this age, we can't even begin to judge "smart" as in academics. It's widely documented that children who learn to read at an early age have no long-term advantage over kids who are late readers. In talking with many experienced teachers, I've found that it used to be common knowledge among educators that all kids sort of evened out by third grade. This means kids were given a wide berth in learning. These days, kids are on a time clock. And judged if they don't measure up.

Which isn't to say, abandon teaching your kids anything. We should all be reading to our kids, playing math games, singing, drawing, and all kinds of good stuff. My point is that we really don't have to panic about education.

- Does it matter if a child knows her times tables but is sitting in her own poop?
- Does it matter if your child has learned to read but can't zipper his own coat?
- Does it matter if your child got into Harvard and doesn't know how to scramble an egg?

I think it does. And I've seen all three of these examples in real life.

Learning at this age should be *play*. Plain and simple. Play is the work of childhood. Especially in these late toddler years.

Have you ever sat a three-year-old down to teach her something academic? The pushback is enormous. Have you ever noticed you have a teacher voice? We all do. And usually the minute we use our teacher voice is the minute our kids tune out.

Our teacher voice is one of the most disconnecting things that can happen between us and our kids. It subtly says, "I will impart my great wisdom upon you whether you want this information or not." It's not presence and connection; it's above and outside the child in front of you.

Our little ones rebel when they hear it. They are all about

look at me. Look at *me*. The greatest gift we can give to another human is to truly see them. Not just with our eyes but with our hearts as well. Often when we decide we're going to teach something academic to our kids, we lose that heartfelt sense of seeing them.

And of course there really is the issue of their muscle development. As I'll harp on consistently through this book, there's a lot involved in play that builds the foundation of the muscular strength needed for the later years. For example, many parents rush handwriting. I see this on countless threads on social media: "I'm concerned that my three-year-old can't seem to hold a pencil to write her letters." I've worked with parents who will make the child sit to do handwriting drills, thinking they're giving the kid a jump on educational skills. A child who can't hold a pencil needs to develop those muscles *through play*. First the child must develop gross motor skills, then fine motor skills. As a society, we're barreling through the gross motor skills, rushing to the fine motor skills. Developing strong core muscles is the best thing you can do for handwriting.

Children develop strong core muscles through play, using balance, climbing, crab walking, wheelbarrow walking. I've said it before and I'll say it again because we as parents can get crazy and weird. When I say develop core muscles, I don't mean have your child do an ab routine. That might be obvious, but again, sometimes I see parents go a little crazy when it comes to trying to give their child an educational advantage.

There is a reason that children just want to play. They are working themselves, developing themselves for the later years. Their little legs and butts are not ready to sit. Relatively speaking, they *just* learned how to use those legs! Why would they want them to be still?

You know what your preschooler wants right now? Independence. Autonomy. To be a big kid. To navigate the world a little more on his own. That is that magical pull against you we see with individuation. That chaotic behavior, that contrary, grumpy *no* to everything you say: that is your little one saying, "I want to figure this out. I want to be my own person."

So then, yes, it is our job to teach them but not in a formal, academic way. The goal here is to help them manage and control themselves better, both physically and emotionally. We work *with* the grain of that pull for independence.

It's much better to cultivate the growth and independence of your little one and work with her developmental needs rather than against them. Let the desire of our toddlers themselves guide their learning.

Letting kids learn

I want to take a minute here to show what this looks like in reality versus theory. Years ago, Pascal's preschool really brought all of this into 3-D life for me. The school was Montessori/Waldorf-y in philosophy without being attached to either method officially. When we visited the small facility, I was blown away. There were the typical stations: creative play, dramatic play, art, physical sciences. There was a tape and scissors table. *Rolls and rolls of tape and scissors.* Out in the open, available at all times in a room full of three-, four-, and five-year-olds. That day they were doing a painting activity with spray bottles full of paint. *Spray bottles full of paint.* In a room full of three-, four-, and five-year-olds. I hope you're feeling the same incredulous feeling I had at that time. Each activity station could fit four kids. The kids were calm, no fighting over spots. A five-year-old took Pascal on as his buddy for the day, showing him the ropes. At lunch, the kids set the tables with silver-ware and pouring pitchers. The bigger kids helped the little kids open lunch containers and pour. The teachers looked on, stepping in when needed, which wasn't much.

When it was time to go outside, I watched a room full of three-, four-, and five-year-olds put on winter gear. Mittens, boots, hats, zippers, buttons. Most of them could manage just fine. The bigger kids would help the littles with verbal prompts. *Not* by doing it for them. This school happened to be downtown and had no play yard. They used all of downtown, going to the public library, outdoor concerts and readings, art galleries, and— this being winter—playing in the snow throughout the city.

I kept asking the teachers, "*How?* How are they all manag-ing this?" It seemed like the teachers barely were "teaching." In fact it seemed like they really were just keeping a loose eye on the kids.

And the head teacher said a phrase in a such a voice that I can still hear it to this day: "Children are far more capable than we allow them to be."

Children are far more capable than we allow them to be. Holy whoa. Yes.

The kids never sat and did official "work." The teachers never gave a lecture on numbers, letters, colors. They spent *hours* helping the kids learn how to put on their winter gear, with the patience of saints. They never stepped in and did for the child but rather gave lots of verbal cues. We live in New England. Having a three-year-old who can put on all his snow gear on his own is worth its weight in gold. If you're reading this book, it's a fair assumption that you are in the upper eche-lon of parenting. You care enough about your parenting to seek help with your parenting. I can, without a doubt, be certain that your child lives in a caring and intelligent home. There is no way your child *won't* learn numbers, letters, and colors. No way.

But these life skills have taken a huge back seat to academic learning. We're convinced that we have to make our children learn. We don't.

I learned so much from Pascal's teachers. They are the ones who taught me that tape and scissors build the muscles kids need to eventually hold a pencil and write. I balked at the potential waste of tape. "But he'll just waste the tape and tape everything!" His teacher looked at me and said dryly, "Go nuts. Buy a case of Scotch tape. How much do you spend on toys?" Oof. Shot to the heart, right?

I remember looking at artwork on the walls of the school and seeing that other kids were beginning to write their names on the paper. Pascal's had a bunch of squiggles. I asked if I needed to work with him on writing his name.

His teacher looked astounded. She took a piece of his artwork. "He *has* a signature. See this?" She took it around to several children and asked them whose artwork this was. The other kids looked at the squiggles and said, "Pascal's." I was slightly shocked.

The teacher went on, "Names are for ownership. We put our names on paper to show that it's ours. Right now, this is Pascal's signature. See how it's exactly six characters (squiggles)? His name has six characters. He's coming into his name. He's owning his artwork. It's happening. Give him time."

Excuse my language here, but holy shit, right?

And sure enough, by the end of that year, P A S C A L emerged out of the squiggles. With no sitting, practice, or "work"; just time and repetition.

Now, of course I realize I lucked into a dream preschool. Not everyone has this, I know. I wanted to tell you about it to show just how capable our kids really are. Just how much they really want to step into responsibility and helping. And just how much they are learning through play.

What does this approach look like in real life?

Go old school, man. Think basic life skills at this age. I also think it's okay to think in terms of *you*. You have done a lot for this kid over the last three years. How can she start to pick up the slack? What can she do for herself?

Life skills are *everything*. Not just developmentally. Not just for getting more manageable behavior. Ignoring them is how/why we are currently drowning in youth entitlement. We have a large portion of kids who don't have life skills. Parents have done everything for them and give them no responsibility. *Of course this makes kids entitled.* They've learned it. Giving responsibility is what builds self-esteem, not saying "good job, buddy" a thousand times.

Getting dressed. At three years old and definitely by four, your child should be able to dress himself. This includes handling inside-out garments (this takes time and patience), zippers, buttons, and seasonal gear like boots and mittens.

Choosing clothes. Let them choose their own, fashion be damned. Unless of course choosing becomes a drama-filled event. I have had clients whose kids will spend an hour switching outfits. In that case, you can put out a choice of one or two outfits.

Helping with meals. Kids should absolutely be helping at mealtime: setting and clearing the table, laying out napkins, getting things out of the fridge. Preschoolers are totally capable of making their own sandwiches.

Pouring a drink. They are fully capable of pouring liquids into glasses. This sometimes requires your putting fluids in a smaller, more manageable container; a gallon of milk is obviously too much, so you can pour milk into a two-cup spouted measuring cup. They do this in Montessori and Waldorf schools, and it's magical to see kids taking ownership of pouring fluids.

Light chores. Most kids adore cleaning the toilet. I know. Weird, right? Let them! Light vacuuming, making beds, folding laundry (badly, but still), putting their clothes away, filling their own water bottles are just a few ideas.

Helping with chores and mealtimes is more than just a life skill. It's a powerful reminder that your little one is part of a big something—a family. They are not separate and special, they are one of a whole. Remember: when we feel part of a tribe, we are more likely to behave in a way that keeps us there, rather than behaving in a way that gets us kicked out. I cannot overstate how valuable this lesson is. When children are *within* the center of your home and life, they feel loved and safe. When we *make them the center* of the home and life, things get off-kilter.

In addition to life skills, below are some ideas for fostering more challenging play.

Physical sciences

Using real kitchen knives and tools. With supervision, of course. You can get real knives with kid-friendly handles on Amazon. Peelers! Kids love peeling carrots! When we give kids risk and responsibility, they most often step right up to the plate. And feeling like a big kid begets big-kid behavior.

This is often a very scary proposition for most parents. I remember seeing a video about three-year-old Inuit children who use crazy sharp knives to cut blubber off whales. What seems absurd to most of us is just a way of life for some. Children are far more capable than we assume. They need to learn about real-life benefits and, of course, consequences. I was working with Donna and Brad on some behavioral issues when a sidebar thing happened. Their little girl Ashley, who was almost three, goes to a Montessori preschool. She was peeling an apple and, according to her, she was holding the peeler wrong and she cut her thumb. It was bleeding and needed bandaging, but it wasn't so bad that it needed stitches or anything like that. Brad was *pissed*. He felt like the teachers weren't supervising enough and he just thought it was crazy that anyone would give an almost three-year-old an actual sharp object. We talked for a long time about why I thought it was a brilliant learning opportunity for both him and his daughter.

We as humans are hands-on learners. And as such, our hands and brains don't always collide. Making mistakes is vital to learning. And getting a little hurt is even better. Please don't take this to mean I think we should throw our children out in the world specifically to get hurt. But Ashley was no worse for the wear. She was in fact very excited. She knew what her mistake was, and she couldn't wait to try again, only better this time.

There is no magical age when our children suddenly know things. No. We shouldn't give our kids access to all the knives in the house and hope they figure it out. But don't let some minor injury get in the way of your child's learning. Sometimes it's the best teacher.

Legos. The perennial classic. It might be time to move on from the big, chunky Duplos to the real, smaller Legos. Of course, if your child is still at the put-everything-in-her-mouth stage, maybe not yet. But keep your parental antenna on alert for the it-might-be-time. You want to start an open bin collection, rather than just buying the sets that can only be made one way.

Marble runs. Hours and hours of fun. This is seriously my all-time favorite things for kids. Be careful to buy the more open-ended wooden sets, not the ones that can only be made one way with directions.

Better yet, don't buy anything and make your own giant marble runs.

Pool noodles can be cut lengthwise for huge marble runs around the house. Add in some paper towel and toilet paper rolls and egg carton "pits" and you will have hours of fun. Building marble runs is all physics, all day. How to fix a run where the marble gets stuck? How can we make it go faster? Remember: the goal is the experimentation, not the production of a perfect marble run.

Fort building. Go nuts. Buy some moving boxes. Save the giant Amazon box that shipped with only a pair of socks in it! Duct tape! Stickers! Crayons! Decorate them and watch the imagination take off. Seriously. We all know the empty boxes get played with the most. Go for it.

Let them take every blanket in the house and build huge forts with marble run moats.

Tape and scissors. Speaking of duct tape . . . *All the tape!* The muscles used to rip a piece of tape off a roll are the same muscles used in writing. You can help your child build the same muscles she'll need to hold a pencil before she ever writes a letter. Go wild with the tape.

Using scissors also uses the same muscles involved in writing. Keyboarding is blamed for handwriting's taking a hit but we can't discount the fact that we've become oversafe, not letting our kids do *anything* risky, so they're not developing the muscles and the gross motor skills that are a precursor to building up fine motor skills. So, really, teach your little one to use scissors and then lean into some trust.

Tinkering. Do you have a kid who wants to take everything apart? I know many parents who think of this as destructive behavior. If you have a kid who is taking machinery, big or little, apart, *let her*. Taking machinery apart is widely recognized as a precursor to an interest in engineering. Putting it back together is even better. Let your child tinker with all kinds of machinery.

Of course, you probably don't want your child taking apart things you need in your daily life. You can go to the local Savers or Goodwill and get yourself a whole box of old electronics. You can find out on YouTube how to take things apart and put them back together.

While at first glance, tinkering may look like your child is up to no good, this is definitely a skill you want to nurture and develop. Tinkering is the ultimate in "how things work." Let it blossom.

Letting kids learn in an appropriate and joyful way is probably the topic I'm most passionate about in this whole book. I see little spirits being crushed. I see parents terribly anxious about their child's educational future based on what the child is doing at age three. And consider this: if you are going crazy trying to deal with daily crappy behavior, here is a holistic way out. When we attend to the whole child, the whole brain, the whole body, we are working with the grain of this developmental stage. Dude. That's everything. The academics will come. For now, stop educating and let the learning blossom.

Play is the basis of all later academics. Marble runs and Matchbox car ramps are absolute studies in physics. Have you ever watched kids with marble runs trying to get the perfect angle to get the speed they want? Physical science right there. Throwing and catching a ball, learning how and at what speed to throw so the other kid catches or even misses?

Free-flowing artwork is a whole other study in everything. Mixing colors. How much paint goes on a paintbrush to get the right amount on the paper? Spatial relations in gluing and taping and layering textures on one another.

I could go on and on but I think you get my point. They are learning. They are always learning through play, and the play they gravitate toward will build the skills they need and want.

There is no type of play that is useless. It's all important.

Our guiding question should be "What can our children do for themselves?"

This approach takes practice, so be patient with yourself and your child. Reframing the whole day into life skills instead of education and scheduled activities can change everything for the whole family. Think independence and autonomy, instead of education. Every family has different needs, so it'd be impossible for me to give every example of how to do this.

You don't have to be terribly creative and a Pinterest superparent. All you need to do is think, *How can I teach her to do more on her own? How can I let her be more independent?*

The Big Takeaway

Pull away from the notion that formal education is important at this age. We have an epidemic of kids who are having meltdowns and crazy behavior when it does become time to sit still later, like in first and second grade. Sensory problems are at an all-time high, largely because we're doing things in the wrong order. We aren't letting kids build the foundation they need to have the capability to sit and focus. We are rushing academics, and the frustration it's building is explosive. We aren't letting learning blossom but rather we're forcing it.

CHAPTER 9

EXECUTIVE FUNCTIONING

We can't talk about learning versus education without talking about where your child's brain development truly is.

Executive functioning is now a buzzword in the formal school years, mostly because our children seem to show an all-time low of executive function skills. It is formally defined as "a set of processes that all have to do with managing oneself and one's resources in order to achieve a goal. It is an umbrella term for the neurologically-based skills involving mental control and self-regulation."

The three main areas of executive function are

- Working memory
- Cognitive flexibility (also called flexible thinking)
- Inhibitory control (which includes self-control)

So, yeah. Pretty much all the things that toddlers suck at. Which is totally normal. Executive function skills usually develop quickly during early childhood and into adolescence. But they keep developing into the midtwenties. When they're younger, some kids may lag behind their faster-developing peers for a while.

Executive function is responsible for a number of skills, including

- Paying attention
- Organizing, planning, and prioritizing
- Starting tasks and staying focused on them to completion
- Understanding different points of view
- Regulating emotions
- Self-monitoring (keeping track of what you're doing)

There is a wide range of how and when our kids develop their executive function skills, but there are also many things we can do to help along (as well as stymie) this skill set.

Let me show you what executive functioning looks like in an adult before we talk about kids. One of the big hallmarks of ADHD is executive functioning issues. In adults, it often looks like flightiness: "I can't seem to get my act together." In simple terms, think of it as "I need to get to D. Therefore, I will do A, B, and C to get to D." For people who have strong executive functioning, this is a no-brainer, and these folks can get utterly exasperated with folks who have weaker skills. It seems terribly obvious that you only need to do A, B, and C to get to D quickly and easily. People with weak executive functioning will drift. They will most likely get to D but in a willy-nilly way—M to K to P to O, etc. Here's the trip, though: most people who have weak executive functioning don't really know it. It's just sort of "who they are."

Years ago, a good friend of mine was diagnosed with ADHD as an adult. This woman totally appeared to have her shit together, although it did seem like many of her ideas never got off the ground. I was surprised at the diagnosis. She broke it down for me. "When you open your eyes in the morning, what do you do?" I said, "I might stretch a little in bed, get up to pee, get a cup of coffee, and look at my to-do list that I made last night."

She said, "Yeah . . . See, I spend a good half hour paralyzed. I know I have to pee but should I pee right away? I do need coffee but I think I forgot to set the pot last night, which means I need to grind the beans this morning—wait, do I even have beans? I went to the market last night but I don't remember putting beans on the list. Where is that list? I should probably check it to see if I did put beans on and I just forgot. If I forgot, I have to go get some. I don't have time. What else can I have besides coffee? Do I have tea? I bought some a while ago because I felt like I needed to switch out from coffee. I should probably stick with tea anyway. I've been feeling jittery. What *is* that about? Just coffee? Am I eating enough? Hm. I'll have to look back on this week and make sure I've been eating enough. Why can't I remember to eat? Wow. I really have to pee now. I guess I should go pee. Did I get toilet paper at the market? Where is my list from last night?"

I was all *Whoa. Holy crap.* That is a lot of thinking before going to pee in the morning.

That's a pretty good example of the difference between normal and weak executive functioning. Her mind would bounce very easily off the task at hand, which was get up and pee and get some coffee.

Of course—and *please hear me loud and clear*—weak executive functioning in our kids is *not* necessarily a diagnosis. So please don't jump to that. Humans are not born with these executive skills. They are developed. Yes, they may not be strong and may lag in some people, in which case diagnostic testing might be appropriate. But don't go leaping to "something is wrong" if your preschooler sucks at executive functioning.

Their skills seriously just haven't developed yet.

Not listening? Or weak executive functioning?

I'd like to take a quick tangent here. I'm using "weak" and "strong" to describe a skill set, one that can be learned in most cases. I do not mean these words in a negative or positive way. My philosophy around any weak spots and/or diagnoses is that they are simply signposts. They help us understand how one person's brain may work differently from another person's brain. They point to how our kids learn and help give us tools to teach them. We *all* have weak and strong spots and no one is perfect. When we look at weak spots, in our kids especially, we also want to look at their strong spots. For example, folks with ADHD tend to be wildly creative with step one of any task or project. Their weak spot may be executing that idea, or figuring step two, or following through. It is my personal and professional view that, yes, we work the weak spots to make them stronger, but our goal is never perfection. I always, always like to work with and remind our little humans of their strengths.

People with weak executive functioning shouldn't aim to be just like their peers who have a stronger skill set. Their goal should be helping themselves be effective in *their* lives, no one else's.

If we look at how my friend functions in the morning, we discover a huge clue as to what weak executive functioning looks like, right? Um, hello? Ever wonder why your little one can't *just go put on his freaking shoes*? Because he drifts. He doesn't know how to organize information in a way that gets him to a specific goal. He doesn't know yet how to prioritize and execute the task necessary to get there.

Understanding our little one's inability to do this will go a long way in helping. Often we ourselves get easily frustrated because, OMG—*why can't you just put on your shoes!* Most parents leap to, "She just doesn't listen! I've asked her fifty times to put on her shoes."

About that asking "fifty times," there's a great meme that circulates on Facebook. It says, "If you have to tell a child something a thousand times, perhaps it's not the child who is stupid." I love that. If you find yourself asking your child a billion times to complete a task and she still is unable to complete it, something has to shift. Your words aren't working. Sure, maybe your child doesn't want to end her activity. Sure, maybe she tuned you out.

More likely, however, she is having a hard time organizing your words into a specific set of steps to get the task completed. In the chapter "They Just Don't Listen," we'll talk very specifically about the developing limbic system and how your child may or may not be processing your instructions. For now, though, it's important to recognize that this skill set isn't developed yet. It's second nature to most of us, even those of us who, as grown-ups, don't have strong executive functioning. "Go put on your shoes" is a relatively easy task to do. Go. Put on. Your shoes. A. B. C.

When we break that down for a little mind, pretty new to the world, we can see that there's a bit more organizing that has to happen.

Go. I need to actually move my body to where my shoes are. Where are the shoes? What is the best way to get there?

Put on. Which feet? How does this Velcro thing work again?

Your shoes. Which shoes? How do I choose?

To complicate matters, there are probably one hundred distractions along the way. Is the playroom en route to the hall where the shoes are? Yeah, good luck getting your preschooler to walk right past it, right? There are probably multiple shoes to choose from. Kids don't quite get weather yet, which is how you often end up with slippers on their feet when there's a snowstorm outside. And to make matters even worse, for a mind unaccustomed to organizing things in order, the English language doesn't help either. In an ideal world, it would be *go. your shoes. put on your feet.*

I know this may sound silly and is really splitting hairs in communication, but again, your little one is brand-new at organizing information. You throw jumbles of words at a toddler, with lots of inherent distractions, in an often crazy order. This is where the frustration builds in both of you. What seems like a very easy task becomes a hot spot in the household.

Breaking down the tasks

We can help build executive functioning through games and real life. First, try to understand where the communication glitch is. It's usually wherever you find yourself repeating something over and over. Next, break down the task: What am I asking her to do? What are the actual steps involved in doing this task? And last, am I saying it in the order it's most effectively done?

Keeping with the put-on-your-shoes scenario, I can't even count the number of times I've seen this in kids: *Go put on your shoes.* And then an impossible amount of time goes by and you check on the child and she is sitting among all the shoes. Maybe trying on your shoes, all the shoes, maybe just playing near the shoes. But definitely not any closer to leaving the house with shoes on. What looks like your child just dicking around *trying* to make you late is most often confusion. She got stuck in the ordering of the process. She got the *go* part. She got the *shoes* part. But she got lost in the *put on your* part.

Yes. I'm breaking this down to a ridiculous level because this is really what happens. I always picture a cartoon with a parent and a child with dialogue bubbles. Your bubble makes sense, "Go put on your shoes." The child's hearing bubble however is, "your go on put shoes." A crucial learned skill that we don't even think about is hearing and processing words in order. Kids don't always have that yet. That explains why we get so frustrated with our little cherubs when they are taking an insane amount of time to do one simple thing.

What can you do about it besides wait? You can start by slowing down *your* thinking a lot. Try getting on toddler time. It does take practice but will soon become second nature to both you and your child. The next question is, How can we help our kids learn to break down tasks into the right steps in the right order?

My biggest, most favorite tool in the world for the preschool age is a whiteboard. Or several whiteboards throughout the house. They come in multiple sizes so you don't have big-ass whiteboards all over the place. Ordering tasks for your child will go a *long* way in helping them develop executive function skills. Lists, lists, and more lists.

Having a whiteboard in the kitchen or wherever it is you leave the house is invaluable. There can be a checklist of things your child needs to take care of herself. A few smaller whiteboards are perfect for impromptu lists. Yes, unless you have a prodigy, you will have to read the list to your child, but whiteboard lists also help develop word and letter recognition. A list makes the task "official." It fosters independence: "Let's check the list and see what you need to do before school." It motivates the child to stay on task, because is there anything better than checking off a list item? I get such immense joy from checking off lists that I'll often add things I've already done just so I can check them off. I know I'm ridiculous. But seriously, kids love seeing that they've completed something. This solution can also help curb the endless litany of "Good job!" that often leaves our lips. Your child will have an inherent sense of completing the task without your having to good-job her as much.

Poster boards with photos can be helpful for tasks that are set in stone. We often use this aid in potty training. Take photos of the steps in the order they should be done and put them around the house. Brushing teeth, for example, has multiple steps. Most often the only one kids remember is *Squeeze the toothpaste!* Yes, the walls in your home may start to resemble a preschool classroom, but that's okay! It's temporary and it's better to set your little one up with real-life skills than to worry about having Pottery Barn decor.

I can't tell you the number of times this issue has come up with my potty training clients. The child will know she has to pee, she sits very willingly, nothing will come out, so she stands up and pees right there in front of the potty chair. Parents just about blow their lid with frustration. Classic case of the wrong order. The child has all the pieces to the puzzle but is putting them in the wrong order. This is where I'll have the parents make a small poster board to keep in the bathroom near the potty chair, with pictures of each step in order.

Break down tasks whenever you can. Just by reading this chapter, you will start to hear things differently. You'll start to recognize all the steps involved in even the most basic tasks you ask of your child. Once you recognize how confusing simple-sounding tasks actually are to toddlers, how do you break them down to make sense to little minds?

Let's break down the put-on-your-shoes example.

First, make eye contact and be semi-close to your child, as opposed to in another room, yelling out to them.

"Hey, sweetie, can you go to the front hall and bring your brown shoes to me?" This task is far easier to do than "Go put on your shoes." I'm being specific with where the shoes are and which shoes. I'm also giving only a go-and-come-back directive, which is far easier to follow than "Go and do something on your own," where distractions will reach out and grab your child lickety-split. If all the stars are aligned and it's not a cranky moment for him, your little one will hop to bringing you his shoes.

Then he and his shoes are in front of you and you can stave off drifting and distraction. "Can you undo the straps? There you go. Can you put them on your feet? Excellent. Can you do the Velcro back up now? Perfect. Look! You put on your shoes all by yourself."

Now. Being real, I understand that's a truncated, perfect-world version of how this will go down. I also know that you may be running late for work, juggling an infant, trying to make lunches, and, holy shit, do you really have to do this song and dance to put the freaking shoes on?

Yes and no. As in all parenting, do your best. Not every exchange has to look like this. You don't have to do this for every single task. There are going to be moments when we will need to do things for our kids because we're crunched for time. But at the very least, notice when your child seems to be stuck. Is it better to spend ten minutes repeating the same demand, escalating frustration? Or is better to spend ten minutes breaking down the task for your child?

Also remember this: this is about more than reducing frustrations in communication. This is helping your child develop the executive function skills that become paramount as he gets older. You'll be creating habits that will translate to "Come home, have a snack, do your homework, then go out and play." Currently, a huge complaint of college professors is that students no longer seem to be able to prioritize their time. It's *these* skills that will help your child develop what she'll need later in life.

Most important, helping your children break down the steps in any given task makes it much more likely that they can complete that task. They will feel awesome about themselves when they fulfill their need to "do it myself!" Completing tasks builds pride and helps curb the ever-present parental slips like "You never listen. You never put on your shoes when I ask. Why can't you listen to me?" We all are guilty of talking to our kids that way and it's not good for them. Anything we can do to help ourselves not say that is pretty wonderful.

This is how self-esteem is fostered—not by mindlessly praising our kids for the smallest things but by giving them the skills to handle tasks on their own.

Using games and play to develop executive functioning

In addition to how we communicate with our kids, there are also games and ways of playing that help develop executive functioning.

Memory games and matching games are fantastic. Don't be afraid to think beyond the physical board games. There's a plethora of memory/matching games online. Not that I'm encouraging digital over physical, but if you're inclined to give screen time, it's better to play games than zone out on YouTube Kids.

Checkers/chess. Most kids I know, even the little guys, *love* chess. And you'd be hard-pressed to find a game that builds executive functioning as well as chess. Don't make the mistake of thinking this game is beyond your child's ability.

Card games like crazy eights, go fish, war, solitaire, and Uno. You can't go wrong with a deck of cards. You can google how to play these games if you're unfamiliar. Basic solitaire is an amazing sequential numbers game. You're building some fine math skills without lecturing. What I love about a deck of cards is they're perfect for taking to a restaurant to play while you're waiting for food.

Board games are key to developing executive functioning. Taking turns is a huge freaking deal. Spinning a wheel, tossing dice, followed by pulling a card and moving a piece—all require an order and organizational thought. Candy Land, Trouble, and Sorry! are a few of my favorites.

Physical play. Do a physical movement and then the next person has to add a physical movement to that. So you hop. The next person hops and leapfrogs. Then you hop, leapfrog, and twirl. And on and on. Burn some energy while learning sequencing.

Songs. There are songs that also help reinforce executive functioning principles like order, memorization, concentration, and storytelling. "There Was an Old Lady Who Swallowed a Fly" and "There's a Hole in My Bucket" are just two such songs.

Story cubes. These are a set of nine dice with pictures on them. You make up sequential stories based on the pictures on the dice. There are endless ways to play.

Digital games. Don't discount digital games! Many parents allow their children some screen time to watch shows. But shows are just consumption, taking it in and zoning out. There are some amazing digital games that are all about creation. Minecraft is a 3-D building sandbox game, meaning there's no winning or losing, just building. Think Legos on a screen. Chess and solitaire are also excellent online games. The nice part of digital versions is that they can release you as a playing partner. While I of course encourage actual physical time with your child, I do understand that sometimes you need to do other things than be a playmate.

The Big Takeaway

The basis of this skill set is organizing and processing information in order. In games and all your interactions with your child, remember to slow down. If your child looks lost and distracted, it's because he is not processing the information as fast as you. Slow it down. Break it into easier, more sequential tasks.

CHAPTER 10

STOP TALKING SO MUCH

Somewhere along the parenting continuum, some expert told us to talk to our children. That may sound hilarious these days, but remember, back in the 1940s and '50s, children were seen and not heard. Parents generally didn't converse with their children. Then, of course, as attachment parenting gained a foothold and then traction and then became a runaway landslide, we all began to talk.

And then we didn't shut up.

Yes. There is such a thing as talking too much.

We were told to narrate our day to our children, to help build language and understanding. And because we're parents and we're always trying to do not only well but always better, we took it too far. And of course, that push to be "educational" reared its head here as well.

Our children's minds aren't empty vessels that we just pour information into. That's not how learning works. They are watching, listening, soaking in feelings, nonverbal communication, sights, sounds, tastes. And yet we sometimes think we constantly have to pour in that information.

I have seen a preverbal child in a high chair as Dad cooks breakfast.

"Now I'm going to the stove. I'm going to turn the stove on. I put the dial on seven or eight because cooking eggs requires medium heat. Medium is between high and low. Now I'm going to the fridge to get an egg. Eggs come from chickens. 'Fridge' is short for refrigerator. That's where we keep perishable food so it doesn't rot. 'Perishable' means it can go bad. Now I'm taking the egg to the counter, where I'm going to crack it into a bowl."

I am not even kidding. I am not even exaggerating. Although I will say this was an extreme case.

The problem here is that this parent is holding his child hostage with words. With *his* words. Leaving no room for the child to have a sensory experience of watching Dad cook breakfast. Leaving no room for the child to babble, start forming words. Or maybe just watch how Dad moves. Leaving no room for wonder, sights, sounds.

I was at the beach a few years ago. Sitting there on the edge of their towel, playing in the sand, was a mom and a little boy. He drew a circle in the sand and said, "Mommy! Look! A circle!" Then—I kid you not—the mom launches into an explanation of pi. Not pie. Which is yummy. Pi. The symbol used in mathematics to represent a constant—the ratio of the circumference of a circle to its diameter—which is approximately 3.14159. Which in its simplest form is introduced around fifth grade. This kid was maybe two and a half. But holy crap, she was going to get that educational content in! Even though the child was proud of his *circle*.

Even though what he was looking for was Mom seeing him, acknowledging his freaking circle.

This mom railroaded this kid's experience. So intent on imparting some early mathematical concepts (you know, just in case this child is a math genius, you can never start too young), she ran right over the present moment with her child.

Now, there's not necessarily *harm* in a small dissertation on pi, but at very best, it's going over the child's head. At its worst, you're not seeing the child in front of you. You're not acknowledging that child in that particular moment. You're not letting your child experience himself in the world as he is *right now*. You are disconnecting from this moment.

Which doesn't mean we don't nudge our kids toward goals. Just because they can't read right now, doesn't mean we don't sing them the alphabet song. And just because they can't read *A Wrinkle in Time* right now doesn't mean we won't read it to them. But to read them something super advanced before they can take it in is ignoring where they currently are developmentally.

The even larger issue here is that you are parenting with an agenda that's not accounting for the present moment. "Being present" is a big buzzword. Mindfulness. Be present. We hear and see this everywhere.

Overtalking, especially in this "educational" way, is not being present. It's what I call future tripping. It's not natural learning. It's not a natural relationship with your child. It's thinking that your child needs more information right now. It's stuffing them rather than letting them be and become and experience everything around them.

Have you ever been in a restaurant or maybe the park and a parent is giving a child a snack? "Here's your carrot. *Carrot* starts with C. Other C words are *car* and *crocodile* and *cat*. *Cuh* C. Carrots are orange. *Orange* starts with O. Orange is a mixture of yellow and red. It's opposite blue on the color wheel."

Oh. My. God.

Sometimes I want to scream. Let the kid have his carrot! Let him taste it and squish it and drop it and lick it. Let him investigate it. Let him figure some of this out on his own. This is a classic place where we have to back off as parents.

Again: railroading the child's experience. This type of chatter leaves the child no room to utilize all his own senses.

Kids will start tuning you out. So they can hear themselves.

What we need to stop doing is trying to ascertain and judge how kids are learning and taking in information. We have *no* idea. Perhaps the way the sun is hitting that carrot is creating a shade of orange that only that child can see, and this will spark some interest in color that will eventually lead to exploration of art and color and shading.

We just don't know. And if we talk over their opportunity to fully experience it, in their own particular way, we will never find out.

Letting them own their experience

So it becomes vital to let children have their own experience of the world around them. To expose them, yes. To talk some, yes! Absolutely. I'm not suggesting we don't talk and teach our children. But we may be completely eclipsing something they see, some chatter in *their* heads by attempting to put words in there.

We need to leave room in their minds for their unique formulation of information. Let them put some things together on their own. Figuring things out on your own brings so much more joy and has so much more sticking power.

This issue becomes especially important as your child nears age three (and possibly beyond), when that individuation phase begins. This is when your child discovers that you two are very separate people. From here on, it becomes paramount to healthy, creative development that children learn to figure out things on their own.

That is the reason why this age feels so contrary.

This is the age of

> Parent: Hey! Look at how blue the sky is!
> Toddler: No! It's pink!

(and looking ahead)

> Eleven-year-old: No, actually it's ultramarine or maybe cyan.

(and even farther ahead)

> Sixteen-year-old: Whatever.

As you can see, from three on, your words about your experience matter less as your child searches for his own meaning, his own words, his own sensory experience.

If you find that your three-year-old is arguing the color of the sky, it's a good indicator that she would like more input into your conversations, using her own experience. Most parents look at this behavior as purely argumentative. But it's not!

It's your child saying, Hey! I have an opinion on this! I want to say something! I want to figure it out. Is it right? Is it wrong?

Is it *mine*?

And that's the super important part.

How do we give kids room to have their experience? To have opinions that are valid?

We need to shut up a little more.

The opposition you may be seeing in your little one isn't always just him being silly (though sometimes, sure) and it's not always him being a jerk (though sometimes, sure); it's him claiming his experience. We have to make room for that.

I am in no way suggesting that toddler and preschool opinions get an equal say in the household. But it's funny because parents often want to argue silly things with their child about what's right in the moment. Which is a lot like getting into a political debate on Facebook. Useless, annoying, and you will probably leave the conversation heated.

Take the sky-is-blue example. I've worked with parents who believe that this is the place to govern—to assert some parental control, to hold that power wand.

> Toddler: No! The sky is pink.
> Parent: No, it's not. It's blue and you know it's blue. You
>   know what blue looks like.
> Toddler: *No. It's pink!*
> Parent: Stop it. You're being silly. It's not pink, it's blue.

Toddler launches into full meltdown mode.

This seems like a typical out-of-the-blue crazy-ass toddler meltdown. You deeply sigh. *Here we go.* You have no idea what the hell just happened. For God's sake, the sky really is freaking blue.

Ah. The power of the toddler to utterly confuse and confound you in any given moment.

But let's look at these encounters from a gentle standpoint. Of course, we always have to factor in the possibility that our toddlers are just trying on jerk behavior to see where it leads. That does happen. However, what also happens is that we run right over them sometimes. Let me just add in a couple of what-ifs:

- What if your child really did see some pink?
- What if your child was aiming for conversation?

Toddler conversation is awkward and weird to be sure, but they do crave the "you say something, I say something" of actually conversing.

- What if your child just wanted an opinion that was different from yours because she is figuring out who she is, separate from you?

And last, not a what-if but still important: Is this a hill you want to die on with a toddler? Of all the potentially explosive interactions you can have with your toddler in a day, is the color of the sky one you really want to have?

What if the conversation went something more like this:

Toddler: No! It's pink!
Parent: Hm. You see pink, huh? Can you show me?
Toddler: There's some pink!
Parent: Hm. I still don't see it but I believe you. Do you see any shapes in the clouds? I see a dinosaur. Do you see anything?

A few things are going on in that second conversation. One, you validated the child's experience, even if it's not your experience. Two, you didn't lie. You didn't pander to the child and say you saw it. Three, by doing that you laid a strong foundation with the idea that you both can have an opinion and can both experience that. Four, in the event that your child is looking for conversation, you moved on very quickly to other questions for that back-and-forth. And last, in the event that your child was just being contrary, you used distraction to bounce out of what could have become a useless power struggle over an opinion on color.

The key here is awareness. Are you talking *at* your child or are you talking *with* your child? If you are narrating what you are doing, you are most likely talking at your child. In the last chapter I talked about the disconnection of the "teacher voice." That teacher voice is almost always talking at your child. At best, your child stops listening. At worst, you're disconnecting and your little one will rebel. Our kids *need* to feel connected. When they don't, they will act out until they get that.

Think about your own experiences. We've all had those moments when we feel like someone is talking at us, lecturing us. There's no back-and-forth, it's just someone throwing words at you. Take a moment and try to really feel that. It's horrible. It's like you could be anyone, you could be a statue. That person is talking a blue streak that has nothing to do with you. As humans, we find this really, really yucky. We all have a deep need to be truly seen and heard, deeply seen and heard as the people we are. Now, we have self-control for the most part. We can keep ourselves calm through that yuck. But imagine being little and not having that control. Or not having the knowledge that we'll get to say our part, that the person talking at us will eventually chill out and see us and allow us to break up the monologue. It's trippy when you think about it.

This awareness takes practice. You start by noticing how much you talk at your child and how much you talk with your child. You can absolutely engage and teach your child all the time, but lectures in the preschool age range will not yield good results. I like to think in terms of less "I will teach you everything I know" and more "I will engage with you about your experience."

The Big Takeaway

Think engagement and connection, rather than educational content. This is a level of conscious parenting that most people won't think about. Connection means really seeing the little person in front of you, not just being a mistake monitor or talking at your child. Remember, a kid who feels connected wants to behave well, wants to be part of your little village, wants to do the things that keep her there, loved and secure.

ENGAGING THE TODDLER MIND

CHAPTER 11

CULTIVATING CREATIVITY

If we say I'm against pushing early academics, then it's safe to say I'm like a professional cheerleader for cultivating creativity. There is huge value in thinking in terms of creativity and the little humans in our lives. And yet this seems to be an area where we often unwittingly squelch our kids' experiences.

As I was writing this, I hopped on Google to get the official definition of creativity, since it can mean so many things to so many people. I also know that many, many people balk at applying the word to themselves: "Oh! I'm not creative at all!" I think we have this notion of creativity being reserved for artists. Here's what I found on Google: pages and pages highlighting the importance of creativity for business, for math and the sciences, and for life! Creativity is not just for artists! It's flexible thinking, original ways to approach problems and solutions; it's the future and new ideas. One of the best gifts we can give our kids is creativity!

But here's the funny part. I didn't set out to write about that. My goal in talking about creativity was in keeping with the theme of this whole book: how can we help our children rise to their very best selves, including mitigating the crappy behavior? And once again, we learn that if we work *with* their developmental grain, we get more of their best selves *and* amazing future gifts!

Here are just a few interesting interpretations of creativity:

"Starting with nothing and ending up with something. Interpreting something you saw or experienced and processing it so it comes out different than how it went in."
—*punk rocker Henry Rollins*

"Giving the world something it didn't know it was missing."
—*author Daniel Pink*

"Just making something. It might be something crummy or awkward or not ready for prime time. If you make something, you are creative."
—*Rainmaker Digital CCO Sonia Simone*

"This might not work."
—*marketer and author Seth Godin*

"Living in possibility and abundance rather than limitation and scarcity."
—*author C. J. Lyons*

Ahhh! Those definitions get me so excited! Kids are so new to the world and they blow me away with their thinking because they don't have a preconceived notion of what or how anything should be. Which is why they do things that make our heads explode sometimes. Anytime you've thought, "Why would you *do* that?" creativity is at play.

Art versus crafts

How do we cultivate creativity, then? I think that in broad strokes, it comes down to expecting no set outcome.

There is no better place to watch your child's miraculous mind at work than with art. Art *versus* crafts, mind you. Doing arts and crafts with our littles is ubiquitous. Glitter pens, glue, construction paper, kiddie scissors—we all have a bin or drawer full of craft supplies. We all have a Thanksgiving hand-turkey craft and a macaroni necklace saved somewhere. The thing is, these items are mass-produced craft. Your child has made something, and for the most part, it's going to look like everyone else's. Making it involved following directions, which has its place but isn't art per se.

While I'm pretty creative, I'm not wildly artistic in that crafty way, so I sent my son to my friend and colleague's art camp. Cheryl Adams teaches at the Rhode Island School of Design, and what happened there blew my mind.

The class was on constructing catapults from raw materials, with instructions that weren't written in stone. By the end of the week, each child was to take a catapult home. On the last day, out of eight kids, only four had actual catapults, one ginormous and not really working that well, one hardly a catapult at all, and two nearly perfectly identical. A few of the parents questioned Cheryl about not having the end product. She sat us down for an art speech and it changed my view of art with kids completely. So much so that I've been passing it on as a parenting tool ever since.

I'm paraphrasing and condensing a lot of conversations she and I had about this, but this is the nugget of wisdom:

185

As a culture we are obsessed with production and performance. We want quantifiable results; we love having something to show for our work. This is fine and acceptable in some circumstances, but with our kids, it's not the way to foster growth and independence. While following exact directions so everyone gets the same results is useful at times, there are pockets in our lives where we want the opposite. Expression and individuality are vital to young minds that may not always have an outlet for that.

That's why we have art. To create and expand our inner and outer worlds. To use color and form and shape to express what words may not.

What a brilliant place to let your toddler go nuts!

As Cheryl explained to us, art is about process, not product. Children should love their process in just about every area at this age. Everything they do is about process. They run like crazy people, not for steps on their Fitbit but because they love running.

Somewhere in the preschool age range, things start to change when it comes to art and crafts. You do projects with an end result. You may find yourself uttering the words "No, not like that, like this." We become invested in the product, not the process. We become mistake monitors. Which puts a huge damper on the little minds working to make the little hands express something. We do crafts with specific instructions with a specific end goal in mind. If our kids get frustrated, we may help them finish it. Sometimes the kids are not even really into it. They're just playing along to spend time with you.

Of course, I'm not suggesting you don't do crafts with your

kids. I am suggesting that you expand what that looks like. When you start to look closely, you'll find amazing parts of your child coming out that are spectacular and not at all about the final product.

Let me explain. Let's go back to the catapult class. Some parents were confused. They paid good money for an art class at RISD and some of the kids had "nothing to show for it." Pascal, for one, did not have a catapult. Cheryl went on to explain that Pascal is a total manager. He's the supervisor guy. I know this to be true. It's not that he's not interested in making a catapult. It's that he's really good at looking at other kids doing the work and helping them find a better way. He's really good at seeing the bigger picture. He totally has an engineer brain and can see machinery in action before it's even made. Cheryl told me he was instrumental in giving the other kids confidence in their projects.

As for the girl who made the ginormous catapult, she didn't actually do the construction. Two other kids did that. This little girl had a *grand vision*. She sketched it and was animated and totally involved in its design. But when it came time to construct, she lost focus and nearly had a meltdown. So two other kids jumped in to help her complete it.

This was a camp at a prestigious art school, so there was a lot of wiggle room. But imagine this in a classroom setting or even at home. I don't know about you, but I would've become hell-mom trying to get the damn catapult made. *Dammit! This is the project. We're making a catapult.* We can mistakenly think, *He needs to learn how to follow directions! He needs to finish a project!* And I know I, for one, have dealt with a puddle of a child after such a pleasant experience.

We see this attitude rampant in a classroom setting. "She has good ideas but can't follow through."

What Cheryl was telling us was that this type of behavior was *good*! It was remarkable that this little girl had a grand vision! In any real-life production situation, you will have your grand-vision designers and you will have your engineers help to construct. And you will have supervisors and managers who keep the bigger picture in mind. To expect a child to do it all is sometimes overwhelming for them.

I don't know about you, but this was a pivotal moment for me. How many horrible crafts had I tried with my kid, only to be met with whining and crying? How many times had I finished something for him, just to have an end result? And how many times do we all limit the supplies and the expression because we've become focused on production (and mess)?

Sometimes we not only stymie the expression but we stymie the control. Art is the perfect place to give your child that power wand. To let him control his own experience, instead of hovering and trying to control the situation. It's kind of mind-blowing, isn't it?

How can you foster this process over product?

First and foremost, you have to let go of the fear of mess. Real expression, true art, and letting go of control means there will be messes. Create space for that in your home. I promise the rewards will be greater than the mess.

Have plenty of varied supplies, not just the standard construction paper and crayons. As your child grows, don't be lulled into "kid art supplies." Buy good stuff, real paintbrushes, the nice colored pencils. Using good supplies shows you honor the work. Bust out the glue gun. Yes, there's risk with a hot glue gun but also so much fun and learning to be had. Level up art supplies.

Be willing to be with your child but find what *you* love to create. You can collaborate. This will not only bring you joy, it will expand her vision as well. You can suggest and help but so can she. Let her.

Let go of the control. Let go of needing an end product. You don't need it. Watch how your child creates. Watch where he lights up and where he struggles. Be willing to help with construction, without taking over. Does your child have that grand vision but now needs help completing? Go for it. Nothing is more frustrating at this age than knowing what you want but not exactly having the skills to complete it. "This is a really big and great idea! I'm wondering if you need help with it, or can you do it on your own?"

Is your child getting bored or frustrated? It's okay to end before finishing. "You seem to be getting frustrated. Do you need help or do you want to stop for now?"

Help out, but not so your child feels the project is not hers. Don't make her finish anything. Don't make her do it a certain way.

Try to create an art space, a table, a corner—a place where the supplies can be left out. This fosters creation when the moment hits, as opposed to, "Okay. Let's do art now." I know not everyone has the home design or room to do this, and that's okay. But if you can, go for it. Because I live close to Cheryl and we've become dear friends, I'm often at her house. She has a whole room with a huge table with cubbies full of art supplies. All kids love being there. They create amazing things on the fly because really cool materials are out and available at all times. It's beautiful to see.

Creation isn't just two-dimensional.

Don't get entrenched in thinking art is limited to paper, crayons, paint, and canvases. Buttons, thread, wire, string, toilet paper rolls, egg cartons, boxes, bags—shoot, probably everything in your recycling bin can be useful. Art is about creation. Not just two-dimensional work to hang on the fridge.

Build actual things. Gather those empty boxes and build a house/fort/castle. Decorate it with bottle tops, felt, feathers, googly eyes. Make a life-size train or a pirate boat!

Handwork: Little ones really can learn how to knit, with needles or without. I have watched a room full of rambunctious boys settle as they all finger-knit. Wool felting, finger knitting, basic needlepoint, and rug hooking—all are moving meditation. Perfect for settling the little ones as well as creating cool things.

Be mindful when talking about your child's creation.

Rather than guessing what it is (and being woefully wrong), ask instead, "Can you tell me about it?" And, holy whoa, listen for the story. You can always ask, "Does it feel done to you? Do you need to add anything? Or change anything?" This gives the child room instead of putting judgment on it. Nothing kills creations like judgment.

Rethinking and expanding our vision of art and thus crafts can open a whole beautiful world for you and your child. Letting a child have control of real creation with real supplies goes way beyond occupying an hour in the afternoon. It builds awesome connection between you and isn't the mind-numbing activity crafts can be (for some of us, anyway). It can show you aspects of your child's developing personality in a whole new light. It's a place to hand children control and watch expression in motion. A place to watch them figure stuff out and try to express what's in their minds and hearts and put it out in the world. Having control and expression can really tame some of the chaos that's swirling in these little bodies.

Saving artwork

We can't really talk about your child's creations without talking about saving and storing the unbelievable amount of stuff your child produces. And it will be *tons*. I have two modes of saving creations:

For three-dimensional creations, including Lego structures and box forts, take pictures. Make a photo book for a birthday or an end-of-year gift. Your child will be thrilled with this documentation of his work.

For two-dimensional work, take a sample. It can be one piece of paper a week. You can bind the pages together yourself or take it to Staples and get it done more professionally. At the end of the year, you'll have a beautiful book that shows your child's artistic progress. You can also do this once your little one hits school age, with written work.

I know that when they are little, it seems like everything is worth saving. Take it from a mom who's been there, sorting through a massive amount of stuff years later—not everything has to be saved.

Creativity and toys

The joke most well known to every parent is "They played with the box way more than the toy." We all know this. And yet, we all go buy the toy when we know the box will be loved more.

Toys have taken a turn for the worse in terms of creativity and imaginative play. For example, play kitchens are now jacked up with every imaginable button and beeping noise, the burners can turn red, and you can buy all kinds of play food. While I don't think there's great harm in this, it leaves precious little to the imagination. I'm partial to the plain, simple kitchen with no bells and whistles. With toys, go for less.

You don't want the toy to direct every action the child does. This is the problem with merchandised toys that are modeled after characters from movies and shows. You child will play within the construct of those characters. They may springboard into other play, but the toy is still limiting their imaginations to what they know about that character.

Most kids are rock, stick, and feather hoarders. There's nothing wrong with letting those items be playthings. Get nice baskets for them. We've all seen kids use rocks as cars, sticks as people, and feathers as decorations for sandcastles. Try to go for simpler models of things that are more open-ended for play. Rather than the battery-operated train set, go for the wooden set. This allows your little one to be the train, the wheels, the engineer, whatever.

Boxes and more boxes, string, wire, tape, pieces of fabric— these can all be good for super open-ended creative play. They engage the mind, the imagination, and all the senses. The key is in having no set destination, no necessary end goal. Not only will this approach foster creativity in all senses of the word, it will also foster deep play. You know what deep play means for you? Your kid will not be so needy. Children play more independently as they write their own story, make their own music, and dance in their own heads.

In any creative pursuit, there are inherent lessons: exhibiting patience, taking turns, maintaining focus, working through frustrations. These are brilliant lessons to give your child. Sharing your love of something, even something you discount as a minor hobby, can create wonderful learning and connection for both of you. We all tend to slip into "Now I'm going to teach you this," when actually, "Let's do this thing together" can be a wonderful tool.

The Big Takeaway

Think learning versus education. Your child will have years to do math problems with pen and pencils. They will have years of writing. Years of sitting and being told what to do. Use these early years to foster creativity. To learn about failure and mistakes and flubbing things wildly. We need to chill, guys. We're quick to try to help them "get ahead" with educational material. But exploration is key at this age.

CHAPTER 12

PROPRIOCEPTION AND VESTIBULAR MOVEMENT

This topic is probably the most important in this whole book. It's sort of the big umbrella of this section of the book: working with the toddler body.

The technical definition of *proprioception* is "the unconscious perception of movement and spatial orientation arising from stimuli within the body itself. In humans, these stimuli are detected by nerves within the body itself, as well as by the semicircular canals of the inner ear."

The *vestibular sense* contributes to our ability to maintain balance and body posture. In addition to maintaining balance, the vestibular system collects information critical for controlling movement and the reflexes that move various parts of our bodies to compensate for changes in body position. Both proprioception (our perception of where our body is in space) and *kinesthesia* (our perception of how our body is moving through space) interact with information provided by the vestibular system.

This is how we move, how we are aware of our movements in time and space. You can absolutely see how these faculties develop in kids. The first two years of life, our little ones are totally spastic. Think of when they're babies and they whack their face with their own hand and cry because they don't know what happened. When they start to toddle around and look like drunk clowns, limbs flailing. As they grow, the focus needed to get that fork into their actual mouth. Within a short time, getting a forkful of food into their mouths becomes second nature. But man! It's hard work at first, right? With a lot of misses. The reason we often use plastic forks with rounded tines is that when our kids are learning this skill, there's plenty of face stabbing.

As they grow into the preschool years, this learning expands. Movement and learning become bigger and riskier. This has to happen as your child starts to discover all her little body is capable of. "The unconscious perception of movement and spatial orientation arising from stimuli within the body itself." Arising from stimuli within the body itself. The body wants to move and discover. We might call this *sensory seeking*, a term currently often used in a disordered context. Sensory issues and diagnoses are on the rise. But all kids—I'd venture to say all humans—are sensory seeking. It's why we need hugs when we're sad.

In the first five years of life, the foundation is being laid for everything, mental, physical, and emotional. Our kids are constantly seeking sensory feedback because it's how they learn. However, there's a disturbing trend happening. I trace it back to what I call the "Be Careful Culture" and the "Be Kind Culture." Let me take a minute here to explain what I mean with these two phrases.

For the first two years of life, we delight in the explosive, crazy physical development. Is there anything cuter than, as I mentioned, a child learning to get a fork in his mouth? And watching those first steps! OMG. How fun is that, watching your child focus and struggle and learn how to actually walk? It's one of the biggest milestones and we're quick to capture it on video to treasure for always. Your child's second year is then full of refining those physical skills. They all start to become second nature, right? I call the eighteenth to thirty-two-ish months "suicidal tendencies." It would appear that our kids are actively trying to kill themselves. They don't know where the literal and figurative edges are. They throw this newly learned physicality at life, with little caution.

Then comes three and four years. They've semimastered their basic physicality and now they're ready for more. *Lots more!* They moved on, though. They have better risk assessment than they did a few months ago (not the best, mind you, but better) and they want to test that out. They are literally moving on to the next phase of movement. Once you get walking down pat, why wouldn't you try running? And climbing? It just makes sense in the flow of movement.

Enter the "Be Careful Culture." It's rampant. We squash all this expanding physicality with a shit ton of Be Carefuls. As a general culture, we limit risk assessment, thinking our little ones are too little to be trying something risky. Go to any playground at any time and count how many times you hear (or say) "Be careful." And don't get me wrong. Of course we don't want our kids to get hurt. And sometimes we throw out a "be careful" because there are some uptight moms there and we know it's what we're supposed to say when we see our kids doing something risky.

But when we are constantly cautioning our kids to be careful and limiting their physical play, we are squelching those "stimuli that arise in the body itself." And that can have explosive ramifications. Literally. It can cause explosive behavior. If children are seeking some physical sensory feedback as to what their bodies can do and we limit that, it doesn't just go away. In comes out in other ways, like in really crappy behavior.

We also have what I call the "Be Kind Culture" thing going on. Let me explain, lest you think I'm against kindness. Of course we want to encourage kindness and love in our children. Always choose kindness and love. But there is a basic need for human touch and it comes not only in the form of hugs and back rubs but in physical play. Which can mean hands-on. Wrestling, rolling around in the grass together, roughhousing.

Collectively, we're so obsessed with "being kind" that we see any hands-on play as bullying or as unkind. We also don't let our kids hash out emotions and social conflict. We tend to "break it up" super fast. This is denying our kids something they need, and again, it can come back to kick you in the ass. I've had umpteen billion philosophical conversations with friends, colleagues, and clients about this. Fighting, wrestling, and similar physical games have been around since the beginning of humans. Hands-on physicality can be really good for our little ones, not necessarily unkind. Yes, it needs to be watched because it can escalate, of course. Like any activity at this age, it can go from fun to crazy pretty quick, but that doesn't mean it's unkind. And it certainly doesn't mean that we shouldn't ever allow it.

Even societies who seem to operate on nothing but love and compassion make room for fairly violent play. The Tarahumara Indians of northern Mexico (featured in Christopher McDougall's book *Born to Run*) are known for their gentle, blissful nature. They seem to have no conflict, no bullying, nothing that we associate with a violent nature. They are almost freakishly peaceful in their daily lives together. But before their famous marathons and ball races, they hold a *tesguinada*, basically a huge drunken brawl. They fight like maniacs. They come at each other like they're seriously intending harm. They've worked it out so they can blame it on the homemade corn beer or peyote, but the *tesguinada* serves a bigger purpose: a pressure valve. To relieve tensions between one another and to relieve the natural pressure that builds up in all of us.

See? Even in cultures where there appears to be no conflict and only kindness, physicality builds up. In the following chapters, I'm going to present new ways of thinking to help mitigate that pressure-build in your child. It's going to challenge the Be Careful and Be Kind cultures. You can filter these ideas through your own family experience, through what you know about your child, but I ask you to keep an open mind.

Proprioception and vestibular movement are what a friend of mine calls Big Play. It's raucous, it's loud, it's messy, and it's risky.

Yes, I want to help mitigate crappy behavior for you. But there's a larger thing at work here as well. Children who get lots of Big Play end up sitting still better when it's time to sit. They listen better. They don't fidget as much and get so wiggly and obnoxious and annoying. They sleep better because they've have this whole-body, exhausting movement.

They also develop strong core muscles and terrific gross motor skills. As we've talked about, gross motor skill development comes before fine motor development. Across the board, with the rush to early academics, we are skipping this vital stepping-stone. We're asking three- and four-year-olds to sit still and hold a pencil correctly and write legibly. We're asking too much. We're putting a big cart before a big horse.

Our kids are lacking so much in proprioception and vestibular movement and development that a scary thing is happening. They don't know where their own bodies are in space and time. The game of tag is being forbidden in schools at recess. Do you know why? Because kids are getting hurt since they can no longer control their bodies enough to simply tag another kid and turn on a dime and bolt away. They're plowing the other kid down, without meaning to. Kids who aren't developing these skills are clumsier and drop things more (aside from the regular dropsies that occur in a developing body). They may not be aware of personal space and have to be right up in your grill to speak to you. They may hug peers too hard, maybe even knocking them over.

Now of course, proprioception and vestibular movement *are* still being developed in these preschool years. So, much of what I just described is part of normal development. I'm encouraging you not to be concerned if your three-year-old exhibits all of these things, but to recognize that it *is* a development and to encourage that growth. Which means a lot of Big Play and a fair amount of risky physical play, within reason.

And mostly what I'm encouraging is awareness. If your child is bouncing off the walls in the house, what Big Play can you give her? We've all heard the expression "Get your wiggles out." We know that if we want children to sit still in, say, church for an hour, we probably have to give them a hard run first. Like puppies.

Know that this Big Play is not just about momentary relief for you. It's the foundation of being able to sit and focus, write and read, have tolerance for sitting still in the later years. If they never get to build this foundation, the pressure will build, and I can promise you, it won't look pretty.

What are some real-life examples of Big Play?

In broad terms, any swinging, climbing, or jumping. These all give amazing amounts of vestibular input.

Climbing. Doesn't it drive you crazy sometimes? You go on a simple walk and your child is on everything. He will find things to climb that we as adults wouldn't even think you could climb. That child is getting intense sensory feedback, and that's telling him what he is capable of doing. Any child who doesn't get that will be sensory seeking. As much as possible, let your child climb! And for goodness sake, if she isn't interrupting another child, let her climb *up* the slide! It's so good for their little bodies.

Reevaluate your local playgrounds. I know in my city we have "baby playground." It's generally occupied by kids four and under. Everything is super safe and low to the ground. Every single time I've been there, I've seen a Toddler Fight Club going down. I swear, it's because there's nothing to climb, nothing that demands that whole body energy. See if you can find a play area that does have climbing structures. Rope cargo nets are awesome for not just climbing but for insane core development.

The Ground Is Lava. When your kid starts playing this classic, jump in. Encourage it. The leaping from couch to chair and climbing over things is just crazy skill development. I recently went for a trail hike with my son. He made me play the Ground Is Lava game. "Ma, you can't touch the ground. You can step on

rocks, roots, and hang from branches but not on the ground."
Holy crap. I had so much fun! Don't discourage this game even
if it's in the house.

Doorway gyms. These are a fairly new product. They hook
up to your doorway in various ways depending on the particular design. Think of a pull-up bar with attachments—
for instance, rings. These allow children to hang, pull their
body weight up, and flip upside down in a pretty controlled
way (for in the house, anyway). The benefits to core development, arm strength, and proprioception cannot be under-
estimated.

Ninja/parkour classes. These may or may not be available in
your area, but look around and see if you can find a gym that
takes littles. These tend to be at least semistructured and adult-
led for safety and liability. Normally, I prefer free play for this
kind of physical play, but if you're nervous and don't really trust
your child's capability, that's okay! This will help you trust your
child and, more important, help your child trust herself. I have
seen these types of class build more confidence and self-esteem
than any other single action.

Level up your outside toys

It may be time to make things more challenging for your little
one.

Balance bikes. Think about upgrading from the easy-peasy
tricycle. Balance bikes have no pedals; the child pushes with
his feet and then coasts. These are excellent for, well, balance,

obviously. But also for proprioception—awareness of where your body is in space and time.

Slack lines. If you have the room and ability, slack lines are awesome additions to your backyard. They usually come with the slack line itself and a balance rope to be hung slightly higher than your child's arm reach. This way your preschooler can work on balance but not get totally frustrated at first.

Crab walk, wheelbarrow walk, leapfrog. Do you remember these physical games/walks? There is an entire generation of kids who don't know these. In fact, some are forbidden at schools because of liability. These three in particular build core muscles.

Wrestling and roughhousing. Have you ever seen baby goats interact? It's hilarious. They are totally spastic with each other, climbing and jumping all over one another. It looks a lot like fighting until you realize it's not; it's playing. They knock each other over and off of things. I swear, I was watching baby goats at the zoo one day and one was at the top of a little slide and another came and knocked him right off.

Huh. Sounds a lot like toddlers, doesn't it? Kids love hands-on physicality. To us, it can be scary because it can look like fighting and it can also escalate. But children love and need roughhousing. Wrestling. Being baby goats. They need physical feedback from other people, both peers and the big people in their lives. Even if you don't feel comfortable with kids wrestling each other, make time yourself to wrestle/roughhouse with your child.

The classics

Here are some classic activities for building vestibular movement and proprioception:

- Rolling down grassy hills
- Rolling on the floor like a log
- Sit-and-spins
- Hippity-hop balls
- Merry-go-rounds (the old-school kind)

A quick note about organized sports. They are not the same
as Big Play because they are adult-led and structured, although
they tend to use the same muscle groups. Big Play is almost
always initiated by children, given the time and space, and will
be pretty spontaneous. Which means the children are getting
exactly what they need.

Kids' nerves are fairly exploding with the need for sensory
input. Again, think about how new they are in their bodies. It's
all *so exciting*. Learning how and what this cool body can do leads
to massive exploration. It leads to taking risks, because really,
how can test your own engine if you're not taking it to the edge?

Just like our kids will push our emotional and physical
boundaries, with arguing and power struggles, they need to test
their physical boundaries. Where does my body begin and end?
What can this body do? How do I coordinate my movements
to do the things I want?

Yes. Young children begin with low impulse control, but
sensory feedback helps them develop it. *And* I think the really
exciting part is that we as parents can have an active role in
helping them get there.

Getting hurt

We can't really talk about Big Play without talking about getting hurt.

All this talk about risky physical movement now begs the question: But what if they get hurt? It seems to me that this is the driving concern behind "be careful" and hypervigilance. What if your child gets hurt?

Now, to be fair, we live in a world ready to jump on mom-shaming (notice how rarely it's dad-shaming, even though dads tend to be a lot riskier with kids than moms). As I've mentioned before, the onus seems to be on moms. And man! You better watch that kid with an intense focus never before found in parenting.

But there's another thing we've been sort of hoodwinked into believing, and that is that our kids should never get hurt. That you are a bad parent if your child gets hurt. You weren't watching or paying close enough attention. You guys, this is a horrible and insidious belief and yet think about it: it's infiltrated the very core of our parenting.

Taking risks means sometimes failing. I want you to really sit with this for a minute because this truth is huge not just for this age but for an entire healthy childhood and beyond. If you never take a risk, if you play it safe all the time, you become afraid of making a mistake. You become afraid of failure. The ramifications of this core attitude affect people throughout their entire lives. Currently, our education system allows for very little failure. Very few mistakes. And I see it in kids in all the years following the toddler years. We are headed toward a whole generation that is afraid to fail.

All the greats will tell you how many times they failed. A large number of millionaires have gone bankrupt before becoming millionaires. Steve Jobs, Mark Zuckerberg, Bill Gates—all took massive risks and had huge failures along the way. Every athlete in the Olympics: huge risks and huge failures.

Risk inherently comes with failure. I'm extrapolating into the later years and larger life because there's no magical older age when you belatedly learn it's okay to take a risk and it's okay to fail. If a childhood is spent being careful, never being allowed to take a risk, it's not as if suddenly at age eighteen that child will go out into the world and be a risk-taker. In fact, the opposite happens. Such people will almost always stay very small in a comfort zone, because that's what they've learned.

For the zero-to-six age range, learning to take risks, learning to handle failure starts with physicality. Risky physicality means potentially getting hurt.

To hover over a child, making sure she never makes a mistake, fails, or falls, is to create a mess later on in life. It's not a secret that our generation of parents is often accused of both helicopter parenting and keeping our kids in a bubble. This is the bubble, guys. This is the hovering.

Throughout this book, I'm encouraging far more advanced and risky skills than our cultural norm allows. Because our kids are dying to be big kids. So much of the crappy behavior is their psyche pushing against being a baby, searching for autonomy and independence.

I constantly work with parents who hover and supervise every action. *Be careful. Do it this way. I'll do it for you.* These same parents fret over their child's self-esteem. Self-esteem is not built on careful. It's not built on the parent doing for the child, on handing the child the answers. In fact, all of that crushes self-esteem. Kids aren't stupid. They know when they're not doing for themselves. You can say "good job" a thousand times, but if they didn't really do it themselves—if they didn't really take a risk that paid off—they know.

Self-esteem comes from doing something you weren't sure you could do. From taking risks, making mistakes, and learning. That's how all of us as humans learn, *Oh wow. I'm a pretty cool person. I did this thing.* I'm sure at some point you've seen the look on your kid's face when he says, "I did it!" *THAT*. That is self-esteem. It's forged in the fire.

We *learn* by making mistakes. It's just a fact. To think that we will learn all we need to know, not just in formal education but in life, perfectly out of the gates, is ridiculous. Think of all the life lessons you've picked up along the way. You learned them by mistakes. You know how I learned that you really *do* have to watch the oil in your car? By blowing the head gasket on the freeway. I had to trash a car when I was eighteen to learn this lesson. Big mistake, but guess what? Since that day, I have never, ever forgotten about the oil in my car.

Even more important is the fact that your child will, without a doubt, surprise you. When we bite our lips, holding back a "be careful," we almost always find that our kids are fine and way more skilled than we thought. They can navigate their risk better than we assume. While they may make some mistakes along the way, they will definitely have some super cool successes. Risk assessment grows and blooms in this place.

Of course, I don't mean throw your kid to the emergency room wolves. I don't mean to say that you have to actively put them in dangerous situations looking to get hurt. What I would love is if we could all look within our parental selves and do some soul searching. No one ever loves to see their child hurt. But is teaching children to always play it super safe going to serve them in the long run? Almost assuredly not. Give them the powerful gift of risk-taking.

When we say "be careful," we're usually not meaning to stymie their growth. What we're asking them for is risk assessment, right? *Risk assessment* is an umbrella term for "watch what you're doing, be aware of your surroundings." We should be providing them with good leads for *that*, not just a standard "be careful." "Be careful" just doesn't say enough, especially for a little one who might not even realize some inherent risks.

Josée Bergeron of BackwoodsMama.com has a fantastic list that I adore:

> Every time you want to say "Be Careful!" see it as an opportunity to help your child foster greater awareness of their environment and their bodies. Try saying:
>
> Notice how . . . these rocks are slippery, the log is rotten, that branch is strong.
>
> Do you see . . . the poison ivy, your friends nearby?
>
> Try moving . . . your feet slowly, carefully, quickly, strongly.
>
> Try using your . . . hands, feet, arms, legs.
>
> Can you hear . . . the rushing water, the singing birds, the wind?
>
> Do you feel . . . stable on that rock, the heat from the fire?
>
> Are you feeling . . . scared, excited, tired, safe?
>
> It's important that we let our kids engage in risky or challenging play because it's a great way for them to practice problem-solving skills. Help them out by asking:
>
> What's your plan . . . if you climb that boulder, cross that street?
>
> What can you use . . . to get across, for your adventure?

Where will you . . . put that rock, climb that tree, dig that hole?

How will you . . . get down, go up, get across?

Who will . . . be with you, go with you, help you if?

It's really about that awareness of what they need in the moment. And switching your brain around to see certain behaviors in a different light.

The Big Takeaway

Our kids need Big Play and big, swirling, twirling, jumping movement. Allowing them the full range of what their bodies can do not only helps with calm behavior now, it sets the stage for a future of focus and sitting still. Encourage Big Play and risk-taking. You might have to sit on all the "be carefuls" that naturally want to come out of your mouth. Physical risk-taking is paramount at this age. Set the stage for your children to explore all their bodies can do.

CHAPTER 13

FREE PLAY VERSUS STRUCTURED PLAY

The term *free play* is another parenting buzzword that has somewhat lost its meaning. Simply put, free play is child-led, with other children or alone. It's adult-free, no grown-ups allowed. It's open-ended, without rules except any created by the children. It really has little to do with *what* is being played and more to do with *who* is doing the playing. In a group, free play is about child-led interaction with other children.

Many parents are equating outside time with free play, which can be true. But being outside and having adults hyper-monitor interactions and rules isn't free play. Any adult-organized sport is not free play. I once worked with a family who really believed that their daughter's three-times-a-week soccer games were free play; they assumed she's outside, moving her body, so that counts. Organized sports are just that: orga-nized, usually by adults. Now, if the kids all get together and make up some sort of ball game, that's free play.

Free play isn't the same as Big Play. It's about letting chil-dren negotiate their own social context. And it's frequently undermined by that "Be Kind Culture" I was talking about earlier, as well as by parents' fear of boredom.

At three years old, your child probably will need some direction, but each year after that you can pull out of your child's play more and more. The key is in not entertaining them. We have become petrified of our kids getting bored. But boredom is so good for kids. Boredom is the place where creativity is born. The place where epically good and bad ideas blossom. Where games are invented, color and light are played with, thoughts start to roam and coalesce.

Just imagine for a moment life through your child's eyes. Imagine hitting the age of individuation. For the first time you realize you're separate from your parents and you have your own free will and choice. You are clamoring for independence, trying to make sense of the big world around you. You're little and don't have many skills yet, so you still need your parents and help and, oh man, this is frustrating. Now on top of that, every single minute of your life is directed. There is no downtime. No time to let life settle. You learn something and then move on to the next thing. You never get to be the boss. You never get to make the rules. Grown-ups are constantly telling you where to go and how to do things.

Sounds awful, doesn't it? It's the antithesis of what this age needs.

Toddlers and preschoolers need time to let all the amazing things they are learning settle in. They need alone time with their thoughts. If we are directing their every move, especially in play, they don't get that. They don't get to create things, scenarios, sentences in their own mind. This contributes to rebellion (crappy behavior) in the moment, but the consequences are even worse as they get older. Kids who have been directed their entire lives won't be able to think critically in the later years of childhood. You will constantly be met with, "What should I do now?" Trust me, you don't want that later in childhood.

But even more important is mental health. Children allowed to have free play feel in control. Kids who feel in control of their body, time, and life are less likely to suffer from anxiety and depression in later years. Kids who learn to problem solve on their own without adult supervision suffer less as they grow. They know they can handle things, because they're used to being in control. And this goes back to the self-esteem thing I keep harping on.

We've not only become petrified of being bored, we've also become petrified of our kids fighting. If there is even a whiff of disagreement, the adults feel they have to jump in and referee or help the kids negotiate the situation. Again, with the pre-schooler age, yes: you will have to jump in at times. This age has a notorious lack of impulse control and empathy. And let's face it, if you're having an argument about who gets the toy, hitting the other kid is the fastest way to solve the problem. Not saying it's right, but you can understand the three-year-old thinking.

There's a remarkable difference in each year that passes. At three your child will need help and reminders in social situations. At four they will need less prompting, and at five, significantly less. The key is in holding off the adult intervention and seeing if the kids can negotiate on their own. In this context, we must be aware that kids are not equal in all senses. There is always a leader, a follower, an aggressive kid, a passive kid, and watching their group dynamics can be a wonderful thing. Taking a step back and letting kids sort the social structure is amazing.

Here's a perfect example. A couple of years back, a neighborhood mom, Jessica, let me know that her daughter was organizing a kid-led kickball tournament. No parents allowed in the tournament, not even on the sidelines. This mom happens to be a psychologist, and she and I are very much on the same page on this kid-led subject. There were kids ranging from age five to sixteen. The younger kids had parents there, naturally, and Jessica and I had to practically tie them down a good distance from the game. They naturally wanted to keep an eye on their kids but we didn't want intervention.

We watched as the kids went over the rules and started to play. Personalities emerged immediately. There was a lot of good-natured "You suck!" There was one child who has autism and wasn't physically skilled. While the other kids didn't cut him any slack, they also encouraged him. An older kid kept walking him through how to kick the ball till the kid did it and got to first base. Then of course there were arguments over plays. I watched nervously as my nine-year-old went up to a sixteen-year-old and got in his face about a play. Pascal isn't a leader but he's a sports kid who's a stickler about the rules. He knew he was right and I watched, fascinated, as he went up against this bigger kid. You guys, I'm talking like red-in-the-face yelling. As much as I'm a "leave them alone" parent, this was nerve-wracking. Within minutes, other kids were backing him, including the little ones. This sixteen-year-old could have given Pascal some shit. But they worked it out. *It was amazing.* I also saw another argument where Pascal stayed on the periphery. It wasn't his fight and he didn't feel the need to be part of it. But here's the important thing: he didn't need me to jump in. The little guys got some arguing in there as well. I'm sure I wasn't the only parent with some blood on their lips from nervous biting.

We don't always have to jump in and solve things for them.

In fact, the goal should be to step in as little as possible. And definitely problem-solve even less.

I could see Pascal glowing because he fought for something he thought was right, other kids backed him, and he "won" against a much older kid. There were tons of moments like this in that one game. And out of the ten or so parents watching with us a good distance from the kids, I can tell you this one game was life-altering for all of us.

As a culture, we think avoiding conflict is good. But conflict happens, especially in free play. Conflict will *always happen*. So the goal should never be freedom from conflict but rather it should be conflict resolution. And that takes practice with other kids. When kids are playing in an adult-organized activity, the opportunity for them to experience conflict resolution is super low. They might not like something or they might have an issue, but there's always an adult there to be the judge and jury. It's a completely missed opportunity.

Now, of course, that kickball example was with older kids, not a bunch of three-year-olds in the sandbox. And while older kids can be a pain in the ass in different ways, they do tend to watch out for the little guys, so it's not a toddler free-for-all.

What this looks like in reality, with toddlers

Be willing to be that parent. This is probably the hardest part. Be willing to hold out your hand to block another parent who moves in to intervene and say, "Wait. Hold on a minute. Let's see how they handle this." What's really interesting is that toddlers lack impulse control and empathy in the moment. But if they cause distress to another child, the empathy does usually start to kick in. They may not be able to be in the other kid's shoes when it comes time to take a turn with the dump truck. But should they rip it from the other kid's hands and cause that child to cry, most often they will try to make amends. That is a huge learning opportunity, one we often don't give our kids. We jump in and intervene. But to the child our solutions can be arbitrary and seemingly not fair. We give external directives that mean nothing. "Say you're sorry." (Kid is thinking, *Why? I have the truck now.*) From a child development standpoint, it's better to leave them be, to see what happens. Children will surprise you every time when they're allowed their own social interactions.

And believe me, you want out of playground politics and managing kids in play as soon as possible. I've mentioned this throughout: it's well known we have a youth crisis—kids expecting their parents to solve all their problems. Teenagers unable to handle conflict or being uncomfortable. Handling conflict starts now! You can't teach this in a structured environment; it's naturally false because of the inherent structure. It can only be learned through kid-led free play.

While you can model empathy, you can't role-play it. There's no point in lecturing children to death on how important it is to include other children. Children need to learn these things through practice. *Lots* of it!

Yes. Feelings are going to be hurt. Yes. Children will be unkind. They must be unkind first to show kindness. If you are ordering and directing kindness at every turn, it's not truly learned by the child. They have to try on being an asshole to learn how to not be an asshole.

And of course, there will always be *that* kid. The bully, the mean one, the one you gotta watch. But you'll know when you need to be more proactive. I am by no means saying you don't *ever* intervene, especially at the preschool age. Our children do need guidance and teaching. What I'm saying is we should not always rush to jump in.

Fostering free play. Start a free-play playgroup. Find like-minded parents and practice disengaging. Let your kids play alone in the yard (while watching from a distance). Build up their tolerance for engaging with other kids without parental supervision. But more important, build up *your* tolerance. This is hard, yo.

If you have the kind of neighborhood where the kids run free, let your little one go sooner than you'd think. Not that long ago, five- and six-year-olds could walk themselves to the neighborhood school. They were perfectly capable of crossing the street and asking for help if they needed it. Nowadays, most people think this is absolutely insane.

And of course, there's just a bunch of fearmongering happening on social media. To counter any fearmongering, I highly suggest you dive into Lenore Skenazy. She is the force behind the websites Free Range Kids and Let Grow. She's made it her life's work to dispel the myths behind the fearmongering that is keeping our kids from independence.

Lean into boredom. Get your old-school ma on when your child expresses boredom. Don't jump in with a thousand things she can do. Let her wallow in it. Let children drag their bodies around on the floor 'cause they're *sooooo* bored. We generally have too little patience for this. Let them whine and bellyache. It's fine. I can guarantee they will find something interesting to do. As soon as our kids whine a little, we feel like we have to fix things. We don't. Let them figure more stuff out.

The Big Takeaway

Free play isn't just about playing. It's play without adults leading and directing. This is a constant progression and practice. The goal, of course, is an independent child who can think critically and handle conflict and conflict resolution. With each passing year, this goal will get closer and closer. Be mindful of this process when your child is young and just starting out on the journey. Build your practice of not interfering. Butt out of your toddler's grievances as much as possible. Of course, you can't throw your preschooler to the wolves. I totally get that. But you can definitely start the practice now so it becomes more natural later on.

WORKING WITH THE TODDLER BODY

CHAPTER 14

MORE SLEEP, LOTS MORE

We have to talk about sleep. Based on my work, I would venture to say this is one of the biggest issues with our kids today. We have scores of toddlers and preschoolers who are underslept and overtired. I go back to that observation from my own mom: parents aren't always giving their kids the chance to be their best selves. Never is this more true than with sleep.

I treat sleep as an actual nutrient. You can go nuts in the organic produce section at Whole Paycheck, but if your little one is missing out on sleep, that food's not doing you any good. Think of yourself when you chronically don't get enough sleep. As adults, we know how this wrecks us: impulse control goes down, decision-making becomes an ordeal, patience goes out the window, we're easily frustrated and generally cranky. And *we* have skills. Now take a little one with no inherent skills and you've got yourself a disaster.

My rule of thumb is always, always err on the side of more sleep. Always go for an earlier bedtime. I have never worked with a child whose parents are concerned that he is sleeping too much.

On average, your typical three-year-old needs ten to twelve hours of night sleep, with a one-to-three-hour nap. Four- and five-year-olds need ten to thirteen hours at night, with a nap of anywhere from zero to two and a half hours. Generally speaking, with little exception, bedtime for three- to five-year-olds should be in the 6 to 8 p.m. range. If you're thinking of the later bedtime, I want to caution you that 8 p.m. means *asleep* by then, not beginning the nighttime routine.

Creating a schedule

I find most parents know their child needs more sleep but usually two huge obstacles get in the way:

One: *the family's schedule*. This usually happens because both parents work outside the home and there is nothing but chaos by the time everyone gets home. Even if the entire evening runs with military precision, you still might not be able to get a child into bed and asleep by eightish.

Two: *the child's resistance*. This can come in the form of seemingly not being tired, resisting by asking for tons of things (stalling), keeping you engaged, or actual crying and/or tantrums. Resistance can also manifest when you actually get your child into bed but he doesn't fall asleep for a good thirty to sixty minutes.

If there's not enough time

Most families I work with just don't have enough time in their schedules. So then it becomes about when and where to shave time to get your child to sleep earlier. Now, don't get me wrong. Don't fix something that's not broken. If you've found a time that works in your house, your child goes down no problem and wakes at a good time, shows no signs of being tired throughout the day, have at it. There's only a problem when it's a problem.

Here's a classic example I often see: Mom and Dad both work, and by the time everyone is home and settled, it's somewhere around 6 p.m. Dinner still has to be made and eaten, and then there's a full bedtime routine. The first place we look to is feeding the child. Not the family but the child. Like they have sleeping windows, kids have eating windows. When you try to feed children outside of the window, man! They go crazy. Seven at night is too late for a toddler to be eating dinner. Most families give a 4 p.m. snack when the kids are famished. And then the little ones are cuckoo during the sit-down mealtimes. I'm all for family meals but not if they're so late that all you're doing is fighting with your child about eating. If the kid is famished earlier, that should be mealtime! Not just snack time!

It's far better to get that child fed the minute you walk in the door. And then instead of frantic meal prep, enjoy an hour with your child—reading, playing games, drawing. Then one of you can do the nighttime routine while the other preps the meal for the adults to eat in peace later. This is for a relatively short period of time in your child's life.

Here's the real deal, simple and raw. Sometimes it sucks to be two working parents or a single working parent. It sucks to not really have enough time. You have a choice with dinner. Is a sit-down family meal more important at this point in your child's life or is good sleep? You most likely cannot have both, at least on your typical weekday. You can try. Slow cookers and the Instant Pot can make it possible to walk through the door into a fabulous meal. But if you are getting crappy behavior around bedtime, it's almost always because it's too late. And if you're getting crappy behavior at dinner, it's also probably too late.

You can also shave time off the bedtime routine. The key is

in consistency. Bath time should be short. PJs, brush teeth, final potty. Two stories. Say good night to everything. That's it. A good bedtime routine should really only take twenty to thirty minutes.

This is all pragmatic stuff here. A frustrating aspect of my work is that sometimes a family insists on keeping everything the same but also wants a completely different outcome. If your child is having a hard time sleeping, going to bed earlier is going to help fix that. That means you are going to have to change the timing of things. That means something is going to have to shift. I'm giving you ideas to help shift those things. If you're reading this and saying, *Nope, not doing that or that or that* . . . well, nothing's going to change. My ideas are just fodder for you to think about. You don't have to use them and I'd totally encourage you to come up with new evening patterns. But you can't keep doing the same thing you're doing and expect completely different results. That is, by the way, Einstein's definition of insanity.

Get creative with your spouse or partner. And if you're single, you have to be even more creative. It really comes down to what you value at this point in your child's life. For me, personally and professionally, sleep trumps all. If your child's sleep is wonky, everything else will be. Children simply cannot be their best selves when they are lacking sleep. I give you full permission (not that you need it) to choose some other fix. If you think some other part of your routine absolutely takes precedence, go for it. But know that you're making a choice and something else might suffer.

If your child resists

We all have a circadian rhythm or a sleep/wake cycle. Your circadian rhythm is basically a twenty-four-hour internal clock that is running in the background of your brain and cycles between sleepiness and alertness at regular intervals. Getting in the right circadian rhythm "zone" can make or break a peaceful bedtime. When you miss a zone, it can look like your child just isn't tired, but in reality, she's skipped over a zone or good sleep window.

I'm sure you've had the experience of having to keep your child up late, for a party or a family event. A child will often go through a little cycle. You can tell she's tired. She's rubbing her eyes, yawning, dragging, maybe cranky. This then escalates a little more and your child may show a sudden burst of energy, good or bad; she seems to go a little bonkers for a while. Then suddenly the kid chills out and you get an hour of angelic behavior. You may even think to yourself, *Wow. I guess she's not really tired.* If you stay out long enough, this cycle will repeat itself. In reality, they are way, way past tired. This often makes it harder to go to sleep and also creates all kinds of behavior havoc during the following day.

Random side note: Every child since the beginning of time will say, "I'm not tired!" Children will say this even as they fall asleep with their face in a bowl of spaghetti. We spend the first half of our lives resisting sleep and the second half clamoring for more. We do not trust the preschoolers for accurate claims of being tired.

When I figured out my own circadian rhythms, my quality of life improved by 100 percent. For me, it looks like this: I'm a very early riser (4 a.m.). Which means I'm an early go-to-bedder. Ten is my deadline. I have to be in bed by ten. I can stretch it slightly to 10:20ish. But if I'm up past then, I've missed my own window and I will super struggle to get to sleep until about 1:30 a.m. That's the next sleep window for me. Remember in the parenting section? How much I encourage us as parents to get enough sleep? Yeah. I can't be up until 1:30 a.m. and rise for the day at 4 a.m. I have to hit that 10 p.m. or I'm screwed.

A good loose rule is that when you find the right window, your little one will go to sleep almost immediately. And your child will sleep longer. We've all been duped by the idea of "if you go to bed later, you sleep later." Not so with this age range. More sleep begets more sleep.

If you are struggling with sleep issues, you should move bedtimes earlier and earlier by fifteen-minute increments. You will quickly find the sweet spot and be kicking yourself that you didn't do this sooner. Of course, you've probably heard of the more standard good sleep hygiene tips:

- No devices like iPads, Kindles, phones, and newer televisions. The blue light that's emitted is disruptive to sleep cycles. Even if you use a filter for the blue light, it's a good idea not to have any screen time an hour or two before bed. No matter what is being viewed, it's very stimulating to little ones.
- A cool room. Keeping bedrooms cool is essential for good sleep. Getting hot and sweaty can disrupt sleep, even if it looks like your child is staying asleep.
- Building in the stall. As part of your little one's bedtime routine, make a point of preempting all the typical stalls. "Do you have all your guys? Do you need a sip of water? Is there anything you'd like to tell me? I want to tell you I love you. Okay. I'm leaving the room and you'll go right to sleep. Good night."
- Cosleeping. I am, in fact, a proponent of cosleeping, but *only if it's working for everyone in the family*. And I do mean everyone. If mom and kid are cosleeping

and dad's on the couch, cosleeping is *not* working for everyone in the family. If both parents are getting a foot in the face every fifteen minutes and not getting good sleep, it's *not* working for everyone. I also don't care if you lie down with your child to get him to sleep as long as it's working for you. However, remember: you're teaching this. I think you're probably screwing yourself in the long run, creating a habit that will be hard to break. The easier, short-term fix is probably not going to serve you in the long run. I also know of a lot of parents who lie down with their child and fall asleep themselves, only to wake up at midnight, discombobulated, and then are up for hours doing what should have been done at 8 p.m. Making them zombies come morning. *Also not working.*

Advice from a sleep trainer

Everything I've mentioned thus far is my standard level-one sleep advice. If bedtimes are a true disaster, I encourage you to get some sleep help. My forever go-to is Alanna McGinn over at Good Night Sleep Site—a family sleep consulting practice helping everyone from babies to adults sleep better. I asked Alanna if she had anything to add about this particular age and she hooked me up with some awesome information, some of which I knew, some of which I did not.

When your children get past the baby, toddler, and teething phase, it can seem like your sleep problems are over. Unfortunately, that's not the case for many bigger kids. Sleep issues among kids around the age of three and five happen more often than you may think.

How and when to transition your toddler from crib to bed

Transitioning your child from crib to bed can be a terrifying time for parents. Suddenly your child is free to escape and roam around. Making sure your child is ready and old enough can help make the transition a seamless one. If she's not climbing out and you can leave her in her crib until at least three years of age, I recommend you do so. At this age, she will be able to better understand your sleep rules.

When you do make the move, it's important that parents have a plan. Make sure you know what you will do if she calls out or comes out of her room. Before night one, sit down with your partner and develop your own plan for when things pop up during the process. This will help you be consistent and set limits, both of which will support a successful transition.

What to do when your child has a nightmare

A child can experience bad dreams because of TV shows they watch, books you read, or conversations they overhear. If your child is unusually sensitive and has a big imagination, she can be more prone to nightmares. The important thing is to offer a lot of comfort and reassurance. Hug her and cuddle her and tell her everything is going to be okay. Keep the comforting confined to her room, so that she knows her sleep environment is safe and secure.

Stop nightmares before they happen. Stay away from scary TV shows or books right before bedtime. If your child is having frequent bad dreams, you need to explore the source of fear or anxiety and encourage him to communicate his feelings to you.

How to handle nighttime wakings

Even big kids will wake up at night—but there are ways you can tackle this problem before it even starts. Cuddling, talking, and being available to your child at bedtime builds attachment and promotes fewer night wakings.

Remove electronics from your child's bedroom. Electronics right before bed result in less restorative sleep throughout the night, so be sure to set tech boundaries and limits at bedtime.

Positive sleep props, such as a toddler clock, can visually cue that it's bedtime and that your child needs to stay in her room. It also shows your child when she is allowed to come out of her room in the morning or when a parent will come to get her.

Setting limits to create sleep rules

This can be the toughest to implement, but necessary. Limits really help in your journey toward good sleep habits and should be established early on. If your child does come out of his room, lead him back again every time, with little to no engagement. You may have to do this over and over again throughout the night, but provided you remain consistent in setting those boundaries, after a few nights your child will get the message. Sometimes we have to help our little ones stay in their rooms by adding a gate or a childproof doorknob. Safety is key, and we want to make sure you are safety-proofing their rooms and installing certified safe gates or handles. Containing them in their rooms until the sleep rules are established is no different from when they were contained in their cribs.

When your child experiences life changes and anxiety

Starting school, making friends, experiencing changes in their lives, and even having scary thoughts can give kids anxiety that will affect their sleep. It's really important for children to know you're there for them. Here are a few ways to build that attachment and ease them into a restorative sleep each night.

Get in some quality one-on-one time during the day and at bedtime so they don't need it when they should be sleeping. Bedtime is the perfect time to build attachment and open communication about what's going on in their lives.

Try a lot of open-ended questions and ask them while you're doing certain activities together, like coloring.

Focus on consistency and routine when you're at home. Children need that structure and need to know that you're in control.

Make yoga a part of your bedtime routine! This is a great way for kids to relax, reduce stimulation, and quiet their minds.

Sleep apnea and snoring

If your child demonstrates any of the following signs while sleeping, he may be experiencing a case of sleep apnea:

- Frequent snoring or mouth breathing (the most obvious sign)
- Constant sweatiness while sleeping
- Frequent restless sleep, from basic tossing and turning to behavior as extreme as sleepwalking
- Grogginess upon waking and throughout the day even after a full night of sleep
- Unexplained bedwetting

It could be that your child's tonsils or adenoids may be the issue. Children with enlarged tonsils and adenoids may be unable to sleep restfully throughout the night because they are pausing in their breathing and consistently breaking up their natural sleep cycles throughout the night in order to catch their breath. If your child is showing these symptoms, it's worth a trip to your doctor. Find out if your little one needs to be referred to an ear, nose, and throat specialist and you can take the necessary steps from there.

Even though they're getting older, some bigger kids still need an early bedtime to avoid being overtired. Children from preschool up to grade two need ten to twelve hours of sleep a night. We want to aim for an earlier bedtime, so start your bedtime routine early enough so that you're able to have a relaxed routine and you're not rushing through everything. I always recommend starting at least thirty minutes before bedtime. Remember that falling asleep is much harder when kids go to bed overtired—which also contributes to the nightly battles.

In my heart of hearts, I really want you to give sleep the respect it deserves. Because it's such a passive thing, we all tend to discount it, for ourselves and our kids. It's really the basis of all thing for this age range. Good sleep leads to a *way* better chance of much better behavior all around.

The Big Takeaway

Always err on the side of more sleep. Treat it as a nutrient. More. Sleep. Always.

WORKING WITH THE TODDLER BODY

CHAPTER 15

VALIDATING FEELINGS

We need to dip really quickly into another parenting buzz-word: validating feelings. These can be emotional feelings or physical sensations. We need to be clear about what validation means in this context: it's recognition or affirmation that people and their feelings or opinions are valid or worthwhile.

Key words: *recognition, valid, worthwhile*. Not: *to agree with, to be right*.

It is possible to completely validate someone's feelings or opinions without agreeing with them. With our littles, we tend to roll right over their feelings and opinions mainly because thus far in their little lives, they've proven to be little whack jobs when it comes to feelings and opinions. They have feelings and opinions that aren't always congruent with the actual world around them, so we tend to discount them.

We don't give our kids nearly the same courtesy as we give other, bigger humans. Like, if you are boiling hot and I'm freezing cold, you would not tell me, "No, you're not. It's so hot. You're not cold." *Seriously*. You might express disbelief: "Wow. I'm boiling. I can't believe you're so cold." But you would not tell me, "No, you're not." Yet that's what we do to kids.

We are humans. We get to have our feelings. All of them.

231

Which isn't to say they should run our lives. And it doesn't mean you are right. And it doesn't mean you get your way. Just because you have a feeling, the world doesn't revolve around that feeling.

Our little ones have a *lot* of feelings, often colliding into each other in their own brains, never mind with you and the outside world. I see two polar opposite ways of dealing with feelings in my work. One: total invalidation, that whole no-you're-not-feeling-that. And two: overvalidating feelings and letting them run the show.

Imagine being told all day that what you say you are feeling isn't true. It could probably make you a little cranky too.

I want to walk you through some common scenarios to help you with language that validates without going over the top, but first we need to separate out physical feelings (sensations) from internal feelings (emotions). Physical sensations are mainly hungry/not hungry, cold/hot, tired/not tired. There can be more but those are the toddler trifecta.

Internal feelings are emotions: angry, frustrated, scared, etc. We tend to focus on the negative, but we should also acknowledge joy and happiness and the more positive emotions. We tend to gloss over those.

Physical sensations

Let's start with that trifecta of hunger, cold/hot, tired/not tired.

Your little one says, "I'm hungry," a half hour after lunch. You know he ate, you know his stomach is most likely full, so it seems pretty impossible that he is actually hungry. You suspect he is bored or trying to finagle snack food instead of real food. Your natural response? "No, you're not. You just ate." Here's the thing, though: how do you know he isn't in fact actually hungry? Maybe it's an eating day (those days when you just can't seem to eat enough—we all have them), or maybe he's going through a growth spurt. The ultimate respect is knowing that we aren't in our children's bodies. We don't know if they are really hungry or not. Right?

In this case, you can validate without fulfillment. "Yes. I hear that you are hungry, and we have one hour until snack time. Would you like to play blocks with me while you are waiting for snack time?" You can set a timer so he knows you are keeping track. Please notice some very specific language here: *Yes and*. That's validation. When we use the words *Yes but*, we almost instantly invalidate. Notice also that I slipped in some distraction. "Would you like to play while you wait?" This is not only good for distraction, it's good if you suspect your child is just looking for something to do.

Moving on to cold/hot. The battle of the wear-your-coat. Or wearing shorts during a snowstorm. Or winter boots in the summer. Toddler fashion choices often butt up against what's logical. My party line here is drop this battle. Let them wear or not wear what they want. But introduce them early to the *just in case*. Think about it this way: most parents don't give in to the fashion faux pas because they're pretty sure how this will end up. Wearing shorts in a snowstorm is most likely going to produce a whining toddler within minutes. *Let them decide* and cover your bases with just-in-case clothes. A yes and a yes.

"I know you are not cold right now. See the snow outside? It's cold. Let's put some pants in the bag just in case you do get cold." Validate and cover your parental ass.

"Okay. Don't wear your coat right now and let's put it in the car, just in case you get chilly."

Validating. Respectful. Covering the just-in-case. Your child is fighting for autonomy right now. Don't fight back. Let her win one. Let her experience natural consequences. A child allowed to go out in the cold without a coat, who then gets cold and needs said coat, has learned a very valuable lesson that will spare you a fight in the future. If she never experiences this, it will be *you* she is fighting. Don't give children your words, give them the experience.

Random side note: You cannot catch a cold or the flu from being cold. Long exposure to very low temperatures can cause hypothermia and frostbite. If you live somewhere where temperatures are regularly below freezing, obviously you're going to be more invested in coat wearing. I still maintain that a supervised quick visit outside will convince your child to wear a coat 100 percent more than your fighting with him.

And for the love of all that is holy, don't fight with your child over fashion statements. Kids don't need to look photoworthy at all times. Feel free if your kid loves it, but if getting dressed every day is a battle, let it go. I regularly communicate with preschool directors who always say the same thing: they don't care if your kid shows up in pajamas. They really don't. If you think about the autonomy your little one is craving right now, what better place for him to express this "I'm my own person" than his clothes. It's the easiest place to let him.

And then there's the almighty *"I'M NOT TIRED!"* (in caps, since this is usually yelled and has been, by every child ever, since the beginning of time). I have no idea why the notion that a child might be tired is akin to murder in their eyes, but it is. You've got a kid falling asleep in her bowl of spaghetti, saying, "I'm not tired!" till the very end. This one is an easy yes and yes. "Yes. I know you're not tired and it's time for bed." Plain and simple, said a billion times over in your parenting lifetime. We validate for respect, but we also validate because it can cut the battles in half. If you say, "Yes, you are tired," you know the response that is almost guaranteed, right? "No, I'm not!" Now you just entered yourself in a power struggle with a tired toddler. Dude. No. Don't do it. It never ends well for you. Just maintain a calm "Yes, I know you're not tired *and* it's time to get ready for bed."

Emotional validation

As a whole, we tend to invalidate physical sensations and we tend to overvalidate emotions.

Emotions are tricky business. Again, having an emotion doesn't make you right. This is where I find things get very murky even for grown-ups. You can have your feelings—they are totally valid—but that doesn't mean you are "right." All emotions are filtered through our own personal lens, through our lifetime of experiences. It's why some things trigger a big feeling in us and not in others. Because we have a bunch of experiences within us.

Our kids don't have a whole world of experience in them, but they certainly have their own lenses, even if those lenses are still developing and a bit primitive at the moment. Let's take anger. Your little one might be totally pissed off because a kid grabbed a toy out of his hand. His lens for feelings are that he had it and now he doesn't. *Ahhhh, stupid other kid!* The other kid is not angry. The other kid got the toy. Certainly it was not the nicest way to get the toy, but the other kid doesn't have a huge experiential lens of "nice," and in fact, knocking something you want out of another kid's hand is probably the most effective way of getting something you want. Certainly not socially acceptable or nice but definitely effective. So the other kid is pretty happy.

Same situation, two totally different emotions going on. Now, clearly, in terms of socially acceptable actions, the kid who grabbed the toy was in the wrong. What I'm trying to point out is that emotions don't make us right. And emotions don't justify poor choices in action. Just like your kid, who is now angry that his toy got swiped, isn't justified in whacking the other kid.

What I often see in families is too much weight being given to the feeling. We want to validate the emotion, but we also don't want to bring down the house with it either. In the toy-swiping scenario, this might look like, "I can see you are really angry. I would be angry as well. Let's take a minute and think about what we can do about it."

What I normally see play out is the child having a big emotion, justified or not, and parents rushing in to save the child and fix the situation. Listen, there will always be a bully, there will always be a jerk. And guess what? Your kid will, at some point even briefly, be in this role as well. It's part of growing up. Validating doesn't mean just fixing the situation.

Raise your hand if your kid has ever thrown a fit about how you cut the toast. Right? A tiny infraction can cause a collision of huge emotions resulting in an erupting volcano of a kid. Your little one gets to have those emotions, but you don't have to rush in to fix everything. You don't have to reform all the jerks in the sandbox. You don't have to make eighteen pieces of toast to see which cut will suit your child. In fact, it's not helpful. First off, you're completely setting up your child to expect you to fix everything. Second, you're not allowing the actual feeling. You're unconsciously saying, *Don't feel that. Here. I'll hurry up and fix it so you're not feeling the thing.*

Ah. But how to let the emotions flow without stopping life in its tracks? Take a break, take a minute.

"I can see this has made you very angry. Why don't you take a minute to settle and then we'll figure out what to do." I'm using "settle" instead of "calm down" because never in the history of the world have the words *calm down* made a human calm down.

There are some super important language shifts here. *I see your feeling . . . take a minute to settle . . . we'll figure it out.* All super validating without running circles around the child trying to please the kid or, worse, squelch the feeling. You didn't claim the child was right or wrong; you acknowledged the emotion, which is huge. "Settle" . . . let the storm calm. And then "we'll figure it out" . . . you're not alone, little one. I'll help.

Now of course this gets trickier with outside kids, in social interactions. Social conflicts are great occasions to teach your child to be his own advocate. Yes, at these young ages, we have to help them navigate troublesome situations so we don't have Toddler Fight Club going down in the sandbox all the time. But what most often happens is that the parents rush in and do all the fixing. The parents figure it out and one kid says sorry and the other kid is happy again. Instead, help your little one express his feelings and figure out the solution.

What's this look like in reality?

Let's stick with the toy-swiping scenario. We know how this typically would go down. Your little one is in a rage because this other kid practically tore it out of his hand. You rush in to help, but instead of directly addressing the toy stealing, you first address your child's fury. "Wow, you're so angry and I understand why. Let's go over here for a minute and settle your body and we'll figure out what to do." You go take a minute and help your child settle. Your kid may be crying and freaking out or just mildly sobbing.

Acknowledge the feeling. You can even lean into the feeling. "You are so angry. That was very unfair." Let your little one vent. Too often we try to hurry up and fix the anger or frustration. It's okay to let them really feel it. Yes! That sucked! Then move on to "What can we do about it?" Often their solutions aren't what we would do. The problem may not need any fixing. They may say something like "I want another turn when she's done." Some kids can easily drop the "crime" and move on very quickly, and *we* are the ones still feeling that the injustice must be righted. Perhaps your little one just wants the truck back. You could ask, "Do you feel ready to ask calmly?" This is where you might offer to help resolve the situation. The point is to let them have the feeling, calm down, and then find a solution together.

The Big Takeaway

Validate the feelings your child is having without having to manage all the other people. Many parents give too much weight to the feeling at hand. Kids quickly learn that this is an excellent tool for controlling the people around them, and remember, control is exactly the thing they are looking for. So let's give them some actual calm control in managing their feelings.

CHAPTER 16

DISCIPLINE AND WHY TIME-OUTS SUCK

The dirty *D* word: discipline

It's a hot-button word in parenting, largely because it conjures up strict punishment, often corporal punishment (spanking). There is more societal judgment about discipline than any other area of parenting. Do it wrong and you're raising a sociopath. Everyone has an opinion about discipline and it's usually a strong one.

Discipline comes from *discipulus*, the Latin word for pupil, which also provided the source of the word *disciple*. It has a wide range of meanings, which is why there's a wide range of parenting styles that go along with it.

A simple definition is "to develop behavior by instruction and practice; especially to teach self-control." But here's a longer list of words associated with discipline:

check, condition, train, groom, prepare
mortify (deny one's body and appetites)

develop, make grow

correct, spank, punish, penalize

punish in order to gain control or enforce obedience

The range of discipline goes from "teaching" all the way to "mortifying the flesh," meaning using a whip. That's a wide range for people to choose from. It's no wonder this is such a crazy topic.

For our purposes here, I think *develop*, *correct*, *prepare*, and *train* are the appropriate words. Our little ones are in learning mode, figuring out what the rules are, where the limits lie.

Discipline is often equated with punishment or consequences. Let's take a pause here because I find there's a lot of confusion about punitive action/punishment, how this is different from consequences, and how both play a role in discipline.

Punishment is a power dynamic, backed by a notion of "paying for what you did." The child does something you deem bad and you will make that child "pay for it." Punishment can seem arbitrary to the child. Punishment can feel like it comes out of the blue, with no warning. The child does something and punishment swoops in.

Consequences are a part of life. Every single thing we do has a consequence, either good or bad or mixed. For teaching purposes, natural consequences are always the most effective. You can tell your child a million times to not jump on the bed. You can give a time-out every three minutes for jumping on the bed. You know when he's going to stop the jumping on the bed? When he falls and bonks his head. That is a natural consequence. What we often try to do, however, is prevent that bonking of the head. The natural consequence feels severe, so we put in an external consequence. You don't want your child to potentially crack open her head, so you institute something external, like a time-out. The problem is, in most cases, the child makes zero connection between the wrongdoing and the punishment.

Stop for a minute here, because this is rather mind-blowing.

What if toddlers are unaware that they are showing bad behavior? What if *most of the time*, they are reacting to colliding internal stimuli?

Throughout this book, I've tried to use many other words than *bad* to describe your typical three-year-old behavior: *explosive, developing, volatile, curious, exploratory, trying-on-asshole* are just a few. I am a huge defender of toddler and preschooler behavior. What looks like "bad behavior" is usually just behavior. It's discovery.

I find it fascinating that as a whole, we expect three-year-old beings to know how their new bodies and developing minds work. That we expect them to be able to control their bodies at all times, control their minds, control their reactions. Three years is not a long time to figure out the mechanics of physicality, and meanwhile your freaking brain is experiencing the most explosive growth of your entire life.

Now, don't get me wrong. I totally understand how your toddler's antics can feel like bad behavior and how they can make you blow a gasket. And as much as my philosophy is based in gentle parenting, the reality is that your child is going to do something at some point in time that's going to need an external consequence.

But before we jump to thinking that our children are being bad or naughty, it is essential that we look at what's behind the behavior. Do they need something? Is a basic need (including human contact) not being met? Are they acting out; expressing a big feeling that they don't know how to articulate? Are they testing limits? Are they pushing a button to see what happens? Are they asserting free will, choice, and independence? None of these are bad behavior. They are simply behavior.

One of my favorite quotes ever is:

"My child isn't giving me a hard time. My child is having a hard time."

Every single time I hear or see that, I breathe a deep, soulful sigh. Right. In almost all instances, your child is having a hard time with something; it could be mental, emotional, and/or physical.

Enter the almighty time-out

Used by many, maybe even most parents. You might want to sit down for this one because I'm calling bullshit on it. I think time-outs are, at best, wildly ineffective. And they are, at worst, potentially damaging to your relationship with your child.

Most parents don't even give them much thought. Why do we use them? Usually for what we see as bad behavior. We need *something to do* when behavior escalates.

Time-outs are a form of discipline. They came on the scene in 1968, originating from a man named Arthur Staats, as a way to discipline without using physical force or violence. Remember, at this time hitting and even beating a child were still commonly accepted modes of disciplining. I think they suck because they are neither a good punishment nor actually in line with a more gentle form of teaching.

Think of your parental motivation with a time-out. Is it a punishment? (He is not listening to me. I'm the parent. I'm in control. Shame on him.) Are you looking for behavior modification? (If I take her away from all the fun, she will stop the behavior.) Are you looking to de-escalate the child? (He needs to calm down and be by himself for a while.)

What I've learned is that most parents put their kids in time-out and say something like, "Think about what you did." Listen to me. There is no way in hell that your little one is sitting there thinking about the wrong she did. And there's really no way that child is thinking, "Mommy is right. How can I do better next time?" It's hilarious that we would have that expectation.

Usually they are resisting the time-out or sitting there fascinated by a loose thread on their shirt or a crumb on the floor. They might freak out because they feel bathed in shame, but that's a consequence not suitable to the act.

The time-out is not really effective as a punishment, as behavior modification, or as a consequence. We know it's not effective because if it was, you'd only have to do it a few times.

Alternatives to time-outs

The big question, then, is how to deal with toddler and pre-schooler shitty behavior. If we're not using time-outs or corporal punishment, what can we do? The following ten things are not in any particular order and can be used in conjunction with one another or as solo techniques.

1. Take yourself out of the mix.

If your child has done something that makes your rage boil, chances are your little one hit a trigger point for you. This is the time to remove yourself. Maybe it means leaving the room. Or hiding out in the parental office, otherwise known as the bathroom. You will have a teaching impact when you do this without having to say much of anything to your child.

This is excellent modeling of anger management to our kids. You can be very clear with your words: "When you do (x-y-z), I get crazy mad. I'm going to take a break so I can calm down before I talk with you." Or even a shortened version of "Argh. I'm so angry I need a break. I will be right back." A few important things to notice here:

- Ownership of your own anger. Not "you made me feel."
- You are going to take a break; when we feel that sudden onset of anger, we tend to say shit that is useless, ineffective, or mean. Taking a break to calm down is always key.
- The last thing to notice is "I'll be back." I'm not abandoning you or the situation. I just need a little time.

2. Whisper.

When our kids start acting like fools, our inclination is to raise our voices and, yeah, sometimes yell outright. This is especially true if our kid is getting louder and more out of control. But there's extreme power in doing the opposite. Whispering makes the child have to stop to hear you. Right there, you've disrupted the escalation. Whispering is also 100 percent less threatening than yelling. In any heated situation, you will meet the vocal response that's thrown at you. Yelling has to be matched with yelling. Kids are no different. Whispering is verbal nonviolence.

Being yelled at sucks in any circumstance. But in front of anyone else, including siblings and family members, getting yelled at is public humiliation. It's really dumping a bucket of shame on the child.

The reason Brené Brown is so popular is that we all have fucked-up shame in us. It makes us fearful of intimacy, of taking emotional risks, of being vulnerable. Once enough shame has been layered on people, they lock their hearts up in a little box; they live emotional small lives. As humans on the planet, we will experience shame throughout our lives. Shouldn't we at least not do this to our kids? And in fact, helping them through emotional turmoil without layering on shame can help them become more shame resilient later in life.

Just a soft whisper, "You are getting very silly, do you need a break with me?" "Please don't push your friend. Do you need some help?" When you put your heads literally together to whisper in her ear, you become a team. The child is not left alone with a yucky feeling.

3. Get down on their level.

There is nothing more threatening than having someone tower above you. It's super scary and it makes kids lash out physically, trying to gain some ground. You can be super effective when you're looking your little one in the eye, on his level. Kneel down in front of him so you are eye to eye. If you feel like you need to place him on a chair to get his attention, just kneel in front of him. The idea is to take away your height, which can be so threatening in an emotionally charged situation.

4. Take a time-in or take a break.

One of the best reasons for a time-out is to take the child out of the mix. This is especially true if her behavior is escalating at a party or exciting event. I am fully on board with this move. But not as a punishment. It's easier for a child to de-escalate without a lot of extra external stimuli. When any sort of wonky behavior starts up, remember: the child is experiencing a shit ton of internal stimuli. She is reacting to that.

Don't call this a time-*out*, though. I have clients use the words "take a break" or "take a time-in." You can walk with your child to another room and help her self-regulate depending on the situation.

The standard time-out often relegates the child to isolation. "You need to be by yourself right now." Nah. That's really not what your little one needs right now. That's not helping or teaching. Children need your grown-up words to help them figure out what's going on. They may need a soothing touch or even a tight bear hug to help them start to de-escalate the crazy internal stimuli.

Frustrated? Take a break.

Angry? Hang on . . . take a break.

Crying? Take a break.

Offer your child a break with or without you. Give him specifics on his behavior. "It looks like you're having a hard time controlling your body. You need a break. Do you want me to come with you or do you want to be by yourself?"

"Your silly is getting too big right now. You need a break."

"I can see you're very frustrated. Would you like help or a break?"

5. Physically deregulate their little systems.

Heightened emotions can be a runaway train at this age. Tight bear hugs can actually physically calm a child down. Putting pressure on the skin calms the body. If your child is prone to deregulation often, I suggest weighted blankets to help them self-regulate. These come in various sizes from lap blankets to full-bed size. They work small miracles in calming the child through deep touch pressure. The pressure reduces sympathetic arousal and non-stimulus-driven electrical occurrences. This is also why big bear hugs work. Taking a break with a weighted blanket and/or hugs can be incredibly helpful for a child who struggles with self-regulation.

6. Process the emotions.

Once your child is out of the mix and starts to de-escalate, you want to address the feelings. Your child acted on a big feeling or emotion. If he was hitting a friend, he was most likely frustrated or angry. Remember: the behavior is the "symptom," the feeling is the "disease." Use as few words as possible.

We all tend to overtalk in these situations. Use empathy and your own experience. "I know when I'm frustrated, sometimes I would like to hit as well. But that would hurt the other person, so I take a break." Give them alternatives: "When I'm frustrated, I like to go outside and yell it out." Or "I like to go throw pillows in my room. Would you like to try that?" Don't belabor the point, just help your child process what happened and then move on.

7. Leave.

Whenever they're possible, I'm a huge fan of natural consequences. In many instances, that simply means leaving. Leaving the party, the store, the park, the friend's house. If your child is displaying angry, frustrated, or aggressive behavior, oftentimes it means you should leave.

I know this can suck. I know you may have planned this playtime with friends for weeks. I know it might be your social time. But this is real life. If you, as an adult, are screaming in the grocery store, you will be asked to leave. Perhaps the police will even be called. If you are having a hard time regulating your emotions, you should probably leave the situation.

Again, this is not punishment, this is helping your child. Of course, give her an opportunity to change her behavior! Offer her a few minutes of a break with you. Try to get to the bottom of the behavior.

On that note, please recognize that your little one is a full-blooded human with a full range of human emotion. And she has not yet developed the coping skills to deal with all those feelings. *You* sometimes wake up feeling grumpy and pissy. *You* may occasionally have a hard time with even your bestest friend in the whole world. *You* may have off days when it's really best that you're not around people. And yet we often expect our toddlers to be on and well behaved all the time. Recognize that there are some days when it's just all wrong. Honor the feelings by leaving the situation or canceling a playdate.

8. Follow through.

I have long maintained that you don't really need punishment. You need to follow through and do what you say you're going to do. This is probably the most important thing you can do as a parent. I'm sure you've been in a restaurant and have seen a child doing something unacceptable, maybe throwing food. You hear the parents: "No. No. Don't throw food. If you keep throwing food, we'll have to leave."

But the kid keeps throwing food.

And the parents keep saying the same thing. Maybe they add in, "You'll have to have a time-out when we get home." Or the ubiquitous "One more chance"—except it's already been fourteen chances and there's no sign of them packing up and leaving.

Obviously, they are being ineffective. More important, the child is learning a ton: that is, Mom and Dad don't mean what they say. Which undermines all parental actions in the future.

Ideally, follow-through starts young. If you say you are going to leave or do x-y-z, you *must* do it. You must do it in a reasonable time frame or you are simply teaching your little one that your words mean nothing.

Three more chances and counting to three are completely ineffective if you don't actually follow through. And in my opinion, that's actually too many chances. One chance is enough. If your child is throwing a toy and you give her three more chances to throw that toy again, that's too many. One chance. The first time we can allow for big feelings with poor impulse control. The next time it must be stopped.

Discipline in this context is an area where you must hold the power wand. Plain and simple. You must be in that governing role, which again doesn't have to be authoritarian, but it does have to be authoritative. If you establish this early, you will have lovely, more democratic years coming up. But if these early years are spent undermining your own parental power, your child learns that you don't mean what you say. He will try to be the one in control. He will continue to push the boundaries in all areas.

When outside the home, following through is actually super easy, although generally very inconvenient. If your little one starts acting up and you've given the warning and things aren't improving, leave. There is little else to do in these situations.

This part sucks. You have to leave. You have to do what you said you'd do. Yes. Sometimes that means leaving a full cart of groceries. Sometimes that means getting the check in the restaurant and packing the food to go. Sometimes that means leaving the party before cake and presents. Or leaving something you were really counting on. It often results in a temporary escalation as you are leaving. It can be wildly inconvenient but the lesson is invaluable. This will do more for your parenting than anything else you can do. It says loud and clear, I mean what I say.

Which makes you trustworthy, even if they don't like it. It makes them feel *safe*. They don't have to push your boundaries, looking for one. It doesn't matter how much they *look* or *act* like they want to be in control. They don't. They want to feel safe and protected with you, even within their acting out.

You will eliminate a lot of future drama if you follow through with what you say. Now, I'm not saying do this once and you're all set. If you start this around two years old, the lessons will be faster. If this is new to you, and your child is a little older, it may take longer for your child to understand.

9. Use external consequences.

I'm a realist when it comes to parenting and I realize there may be situations that you can't just leave. Though honestly, those times are far more rare than you'd probably like to admit. There are going to be times when natural consequences aren't enough. There are going to be lots of times your child starts to escalate and you're home and you can't just leave. For some kids, you will need an external consequence.

I want to be super clear here because this is an idea that I've been circling throughout this book and it's a place where parents get mucked up. There will be times when you need to assert your parental power. You must. You must be the one in control because someone always is in control. And if it's not you, it's your child, who has limited control, impulses, and basic knowledge. This does not make you mean. This makes you the smarter, more experienced person in control of the situation.

I find many parents have a base philosophy of trying to be equitable and fair. You can be the best, most loving, gentle parent in the world and there will come a time when you lose control of the situation. When you need to rein things in and fast. External consequences have a time and a place. The trick is in doing them well.

DON'T

- Don't make empty threats; don't threaten something you won't do. If you aren't going to leave the party, don't threaten it. For the love of all that is holy, don't threaten ginormous things you have no intention of doing. A common one is "You won't be able to come to Disney with us if you keep doing that." Are you really going to leave your three-year-old home from Disney?

- Don't threaten something off in the future. If you feel the need to give a consequence in the moment, it must be in the moment. There has to be a direct cause and effect—otherwise it is useless. Don't threaten "No dessert after dinner" in the morning. Or "No swim class tomorrow." Your child won't track that.

- Don't bribe in the throes of inappropriate behavior. "If you stop doing that you can have another piece of cake." Little kids may have very low impulse control but they're smart AF. They get hip to bribery and what they need to do to get it real fast.

DO

- An external consequence at this age *has* to be swift/immediate, small, and fitting the "crime." The closer this is to real life, the better.
- Take away items. If they are throwing blocks, the blocks get taken. If they are dropping food at a a restaurant, take the food away.
- Toy time-outs. If you need to give a chance, give it with warning. "Hey, if you hit one more time, I'm going to put your train on the fridge."
- Shut off electronics. If your child is being a pill while watching TV, shut it off.

10. Use your mom/dad voice.

I call this your mom voice, but of course it could be your dad voice. Here's the thing. Dads and males in general have this voice already. They have a lower, sometimes booming pitch. They generally use a shit ton fewer words than females. A dad can say, "Cut the crap," and the kid just does. This isn't due to any great issue the child has with either parent. Men generally put up with less shit. And men in general are really good at expressing when they've had enough. We as women should take a lesson from the dads.

This voice should be firm, have a low pitch, use zero baby-talk affectation, and—this is most important—never end with a question mark. Be mindful how you speak. Are you asking your child to stop being a whack job? Or are you telling him? Is your voice super high-pitched, even squeaky? I'm pretty against baby-talk affectation anyway, except maybe in the first year when they really can't do any wrong. I'm talking about the singsong way many people talk to their children. It's saccharine-sweet and high-pitched, and it goes up in inflection at the end of the sentence.

If you're a "Good job!" sayer, you probably say it in this voice. You don't have to talk like that to children. They are craving autonomy and are trying to find their place, and that includes respect. Respect them by using the same tone you'd use with older people. Using that baby singsong voice is infantilizing them and can even be condescending.

But mostly, it's terribly ineffective if you are using that voice to try to stop or change inappropriate behavior. A firm voice doesn't mean that you are yelling or being mean. It says, *I mean business here*. Cultivate that voice in your parenting.

Note: Everything in this chapter and book is geared toward average issues in the neurotypical child. Almost every toddler and preschooler is going to throw an epic fit at some point or another. If you feel like your situation with your little one is above and beyond what I'm describing here, please seek help. If your child doesn't respond to taking breaks and normal consequences, there may be a larger issue at play. For example, if your little one reacts so explosively that she becomes a danger to herself, you, or siblings, it's time to get some help.

The Big Takeaway

This chapter is not the be-all and end-all in managing toddler behavior. The subtitle on this book cover specifically mentions "without time-outs." I know how dealing with behavior gets all kinds of sketchy. This whole book really is about shifting your thinking, shifting your ideas of parenting, shifting your environment so that you can mitigate typical "bad" behavior before getting to the point of feeling like you have to come down super hard on your child. What's going on is almost never really about the obvious behavior you're seeing. Look for what's underneath the behavior.

CHAPTER 17

THEY JUST DON'T LISTEN

I'd say one the biggest complaints I hear from parents is "I can't get him to listen to me!" There are certainly times when our kids flat-out ignore us. And there are certainly times when our kids look us right in the eye and don't do what we ask of them. Or do the opposite. But I also find that there's a huge communication gap between grown-ups and little ones and there's a couple of reasons why. One, we don't give our kids the time they need to actually process information and respond. Two, we overlook just how underdeveloped some parts of the brain are at this age. We expect our preschooler to listen and respond in way that's not really appropriate to where they are developmentally.

It can take a toddler up to forty-five seconds to actually hear your words. Then, because of still-developing executive function skills and limbic systems, it takes time for them to actually sort the words in a meaningful way. That's a really long time to process one directive!

We also stymie an already slow process by simply talking too much, particularly when we're asking our kids to listen and respond, usually to a request (clean up, come here, put on your shoes, etc.). Too often we are simply using too many words.

Developing limbic systems

The limbic system is "a complex system of nerves and networks in the brain, involving several areas near the edge of the cortex concerned with instinct and mood. It controls the basic emotions (fear, pleasure, anger) and drives (hunger, sex, dominance, care of offspring)." It is linked with executive functioning; how we process and order information can affect the response from our limbic system.

Shaving language is a term I came up with years ago in my potty training work. As I discussed in the executive functioning chapter, our kids are in the early stages of processing language. Their limbic systems are still developing, making their emotional responses to external and internal stimuli wonky AF.

They simply can't hear and respond to too many words or the internal stimuli go nuts. I've discussed talking too much already in the context of railroading our kids' experience. I don't mean to say we should only ever be using short sentences with doable directives. Using rich language is important for developing minds. However, we do have to be cautious when we need our kids to do a particular thing or really listen to what we are saying. Too many words and rich descriptive language will simply not be effective.

With the developing executive functioning and limbic systems, kids move slowly and react quickly. It takes them a long time to hear the words you are saying, put them in order, and then physically respond to the message. If you muck up your intention with a bunch of other words, it gets very confusing and your little one will freeze up. Or not hear you. Or act like she hasn't heard you. Or completely overreact.

I can't count the number of times I've worked with a family in which the mom feels like the dad is more effective. Or the parents think there's something seriously amiss with the mom–child relationship because the dad never seems to have an issue. Of course, this isn't always the case but it is often enough to be significant. You know why? Men, in general, talk less. They have a tendency to be very direct. Firm. No nonsense. But most important, they tend not to say extraneous words. This makes them more effective in certain circumstances.

Women, myself included, have a tendency to have a thousand browser bars open at all times in our minds. And we're tracking them all. And we feel the need to explain everything about everything.

Women have a more pronounced limbic system than men. This can mean that women are more sensitive in evaluating social and interpersonal relations. Not only are we sensitive to them but we're going to share everything we know about them with you, even if you don't want to hear it.

Men tend to think more mathematically, in a direct and linear way. I first started noticing this in potty training, where the myth "boys are harder to train than girls" still, to this day, prevails. I couldn't for the life of me figure out why that would be true. Over the years, I realized that most of the time (though this is rapidly changing) little boys are potty trained by females. And I also realized that many, if not most, boys responded much better to shorter directives without a lot of added chatter. I attended a Brain Fair at a local university, and lo and behold, they showed a 3-D very cool image of the brain and the professor laughingly harped on the difference between men's and women's limbic systems.

None of this is a judgment, but it goes a long way toward explaining how our communication can be so vastly different and also so misunderstood. Because our children are still developing, they can't keep up with the executive functioning and limbic system of a grown woman. And that would be Mom. Generally speaking, we women talk too much and too fast for our kids and our men to track us. Which makes perfect sense! I asked Pascal if this was his experience and it was like I'd opened a portal of understanding. His constant "Wait. What?" isn't him being a twelve-year-old boy not listening to me. It's me. I slaughter him with words. Well, now I'm aware, so I'm working on it.

If you are a woman reading this, start paying attention to how much information you give. In almost every instance when I've brought this to a couple's attention, every person says, *Yes.*

It looks like this: You really do need to leave the house in the next five minutes and you want your little one to put on his shoes.

"Sweetie! It's eight twenty-five, we have to go! If we don't get in the car in the next five minutes, Mommy's going to be late for work. You don't want me to be late for work, do you? My boss will be angry with me and I don't like that. Can you please put on your shoes like I asked you to do five minutes ago?" Your child's reaction may be to freeze up (ignore you) or go bonkers.

It's often because there's way too much language there! What is the task you'd like your child to do? *Go directly to that task. Do not pass Go.* Your three-year-old has zero concept of being late, of having a job, of your boss, whom he never sees. *Shoes on*. Those are the only words he needs. He can't track all that information. If you throw too many words at a child, he hears a meaningless jumble. Then of course he can't complete the thing you've asked of him.

This isn't to say that we shouldn't use lots of language in other areas. I'm in no way suggesting that we dumb our kids down. Nor am I suggesting that anything is wrong with our men. I'm just talking about information overload. And we all know, by virtue of having the internet, how powerful information overload can be. It paralyzes us. Our brains hit a point of saturation and things just freeze. With our little ones, it can also trigger a freak-out response.

As with everything else in this book, use this as tool. Practice. If you're a mom, ask your partner and your kids, "Do I say too many things? Do I talk too fast?" If you're a man, tell your partner when she's overloading. Get comfortable with a sign, like a *T* for time-out or something. "Honey, too much. What are you asking me?" This is a fabulous tool for your toolbox. Try to catch each other in the moment. You can get really good at this, both of you, and it becomes amazing.

A really good rule of thumb is to be aware that a three-year-old's brain and your average dog's brain have almost exactly the same level of development. Of course, our kids quickly surpass the dog. But think of how effective it would be to direct a dog with as much talk as we attempt to direct our kids. It becomes laughable. Yes, we talk to dogs all the time with love and lots of language. But when it's time to sit or come, we don't use all the words. We use the most basic words for the task at hand.

Of course, you don't have to bark commands at your little one like you might with a dog. But I find it's an excellent gauge for judging the sheer amount of language you use.

Bridging attention

Now let's talk about another form of "not listening": when your child is playing or involved in something and just doesn't listen. She is entrenched in what she's doing and seems to think ignoring you will make you just go away.

While it's certainly possible that she may actually be ignoring you and wishing you'd just go away, let's first make sure she is actually hearing you. Many of us leap to the conclusion that our kids are intentionally not listening and we glide right over the fact that they literally might not be hearing us.

A wonderful and amazing developmental change happens around three years old and continues into the fourth and fifth year. Your child's play changes. Children at this point move from parallel to cooperative play. They also start going into *deep play*. Deep play is a spectacular thing. They get into it, they get lost . . . they *become* the thing they're playing. This looks almost like the polar opposite of Big Play. This is introspective and imaginative. And very developmentally appropriate. Now imagine yourself lost in thought and multiply that by a hundred. Add on the fact that you have no adult responsibilities pulling you back to reality. You're gone, man . . . You're off on some wild adventure in your head.

This is where your preschooler is at. *It's wonderful.* It also creates a remarkable lack of hearing. To communicate, we have to pull the child out of the play, out of his head, out of the grand adventure.

All too often, though, what happens is we don't recognize that this is happening or we don't realize how far away the children really are. So we yell from the kitchen, "Time to eat!"

260

Shoot, we may even yell it three or four times, and then we get super aggravated when they don't respond. Before you lose your shit *again* for this, here are a few things you can do to ensure they are actually hearing you.

1. *Make sure you make eye contact.* This means going to the child, getting down on his level, and making eye contact. Almost all of us are in the habit of calling from another room. Or even the same room. But if you don't make eye contact, getting a sort of nonverbal confirmation that your little one has heard you, your words have probably skimmed right past his ears.

2. *Give them that time.* Prepare them, give the warning prompts, set the timer. Don't expect your child to jump out of deep play and respond; really don't expect them to jump out happily. In fact, you can probably expect some annoyance. One of the things I hate about our general treatment of children is that we don't give them the same courtesies as we give all other humans. Imagine you're reading the best book of your life, an absolute page-turner. I call from the other room, "We gotta go in five minutes!" You might hear my voice as a blur in the background but your mind isn't budging. I'm irritated with you, so I come into the room and say, "Hey! I said let's go!"

Now imagine me taking the book out of your hand and saying in a snotty voice, "You are not listening to me!"

Dude. If this was two grown-ups, you'd probably clock me. You can't come up on someone lost in an activity and expect an immediate response. You *really* can't expect an immediate *good* response. Yet we consistently do this to our kids and we do expect them to just jump to it. Give them time to process. Give them time to come out of the deep play.

3. *Bridge their attention.* This works phenomenally well with both digital and real-life play. It's important to remember with digital devices, whether it's a show or a game, that your child is *in it.* Not an observer but *in* the screen. Same with real-life play. The best way to get children back to the real world is to enter their world and lead them out.

When your child is immersed in something, go be with her for a minute or two. Sit right by her, watching what she's watching, whether it's a screen or real play. See if you can see where she's at. After a minute or two, ask her a question about what she's seeing, about what's going on in her head. Usually you'll get a spacey reply; her voice may sound distracted and off in the distance. Keep talking and asking questions until her voice sounds more in the present. Then say, "Okay, after x-y-z, it's time to shut down the iPad (or put the dolls to bed, or whatever it is)."

I was working with a dad whose little guy couldn't pull himself away from trains. The parents almost wanted to ban trains in the house because this kid would lose so much focus in the real world that getting him to exit train play was nearing impossible. When the dad started bridging his attention, even he was amazed. "He's the wheels! He's actually the train itself! It's so cool!" *Yes.* And Dad succeeded in pulling this kid out of the trains. Sure, it took about ten minutes, but it completely worked.

This is really important, so I'm saying it more than once and in many different ways: I've had parents sort of freak out that they don't really have that time. Calculate the time it takes to get your child motivated with the old method of calling across the house, your getting aggravated, and the ensuing drama. I'm sure you're easily losing ten minutes anyway.

And consider this: Do you want to lose ten minutes in getting frustrated with your kid? Or lose ten minutes showing interest in what your child is doing? With that dad and son, a wonderful thing began to unfold. The child was thrilled that his dad was showing so much interest in what he was doing. Seeing and acknowledging our kids' deep play is so freaking validating for them. It's a beautiful thing.

4. Help them close out the activity. Even with timers and many prompts, preschoolers don't have a sense of time. We often give two-minute warnings, five-minute warnings. But these can be senseless if the children aren't in fact *done* with their play. Go back to the grown-up example with the book. Most of us love to stop reading at the end of a chapter or a break in the chapter. At the very least, we read till the current action stops. Same goes with kids and play. Rather than give time warnings, help them close out the activity.

> "Okay, one more trip around the track and the trains go back to the wheelhouse."
> "Let's feed the baby (doll) one last time and put her to sleep."
> "Build the tower one more time and then the blocks go back in the basket."
> "Finish this last game and the iPad goes to sleep for a while."

You get the idea. This helps the child finish the play instead of having to drop everything in the middle of things. It's also super respectful.

The Big Takeaway

Don't assume your child isn't listening. You may be using too many words for them to unscramble the message in the time you are expecting. Use fewer words, more eye contact, and above all, connection when it seems like your little one isn't listening. And remember, these are long-term tools that take patience and practice on your part.

UNDERSTANDING TODDLER BEHAVIOR

CHAPTER 18

TRANSITIONS AND PREPARING THE CHILD

I'm going to piggyback right off the last chapter to talk more about transitions. They may be one of the hardest parts of being a little kid in a big world. Grown-ups move *fast*. We move from one thing to another very quickly. Most of us, by adulthood, have developed strong executive function skills or, at the very least, ones that work for us. We can prioritize and sort information incredibly fast.

We can cook breakfast while simultaneously thinking about necessary items in backpacks, about when we can slip in a load of laundry, what the traffic might be like, is our favorite barista at the coffee shop today, and did I put that paperwork in my bag? We also are very good about finding shoes and putting them on. We may lose our keys and our shit sometimes, but generally speaking, we can plan our next moves with ease.

Our little ones cannot. They are literally incapable. Unless they were born with a freakish amount of executive functioning skills and a fully developed limbic system (trust me, they weren't), chances are they need a lot of time to process and execute transitions.

Transitions can be little and they can be huge. We have many transitions in a day. Leaving the house to go somewhere, arriving anywhere (even super fun places are still a transition), going from playing to eating to nap/bedtime—all transitions. And of course, we sometimes have huge transitions. Moving, big vacations, developmental milestones, new schools, and divorce/ separation are the most common. I've maintained for years that children who struggle with potty training are most often strug- gling with the abrupt transition, not the actual potty training.

I'm sure you're very well aware that some transitions are easier than others. This can be because of the overall temper- ament of your child or maybe even the daily temperament. Pleasant transitions are always easier. Have your child go put on his shoes to leave the house for a haircut. Do the same to go out for ice cream. It doesn't take a rocket scientist to figure out which one will be easier.

One of the most common problems I see parents struggling with is transitions. Getting home from a long day of school and work creates huge drama. Leaving the park causes a tantrum. Your child doesn't want to quit playing and sit down for dinner, making the family meal a disaster. Look through your day and see if this is true for you. It may not be, but see if you can find a pattern of drama at transitions. I'm betting you can.

Making transitions smoother and easier

The first thing, as always, is recognizing how their little brains work. As I've said, it can take up to forty-five seconds for a child to actually hear and process your words. And even then the words may be a little jumbled. So they often don't move very fast upon hearing our words. It also takes them more than a minute to get used to the idea that they are being expected to move on.

I'd say we generally know this to be true since the "five-minute warning" is ubiquitous among the toddler parenting crowd. But that still may not be enough time. Your child may need several promptings and warnings, so it's essential that you build in that time. Be prepared for it. As much as humanly possible—and I know that it's not always possible at all—give yourself a good buffer of time to factor in that delay. Know that if you have to leave at, say, 8:30 a.m., you should start warnings sometimes as early as eight.

This often means slowing down your life by a lot. As we've discussed, we can fall into keeping our family and selves so busy that we don't allow for these slow transition times. Here's the funny part. When I'm working with a family on slowing down transition times, I'm often met with "I don't have time to move that slowly in the morning!" But the reason they started with me is that their that little one is causing so much drama that they can't ever leave the house on time.

There are a few tools I have that can help prepare your little one for transitions.

Use whiteboards

As I said in chapter 9, "Executive Functioning," I'm a huge fan of whiteboards. I personally have three in my house. You can buy big ones or little ones and have them all over the house if you so desire.

I like having a whiteboard list by the door, with checklists of what the child might need to leave. I like having one in the child's bedroom so he knows what he's doing in the morning, maybe including the bathroom routine.

Of course, your little one probably can't read yet, but that's okay! If you write the list with your child, she will follow along with the words. If you'd like to draw a little picture to go with it, that's cool too. I like whiteboards because kids *love* to cross off or erase the list. It's also easy to change the list for days when the routine is different.

Think of any transitions that seem particularly hard. Break down all the things that might be happening, including any hot spots your child may have, and write a list.

When I started working with Kayla and Jon, their little guy Marcus was clearly butting up against fast transitions. His tantrums almost always happened when they were leaving or arriving somewhere. When we plotted out more preparation for Marcus, Kayla got very panicky. "That's so much work! I don't have time!" Here's the thing I reiterated in the last chapter: they were regularly losing double that time when Marcus would melt down. If you're spending a good amount of time putting out toddler fires, let's put the work into preventing them.

Kayla started using a few whiteboards around the house. She went over the day with Marcus so he could know what to expect. She left ample time for leaving the house and leaving activities. Once Marcus knew what was coming, his tantrums eased up a lot. He just needed time and to know what was coming, in what order.

What can seem like easy, normal tasks to us as grown-ups can feel overwhelming to little ones who don't have executive functioning skills yet and whose limbic systems aren't fully developed. Everything seems like a jumble and oftentimes way too rushed for them. Breaking down the things that go into a transition like this can slow things down into doable chunks.

This also fosters autonomy. Most kids start to memorize their list, so they're "reading" it. Then they start going through the list themselves. This takes you out of nagging and saying things a billion times.

Verbally prepare the transition

Now, of course you can't carry a whiteboard with you everywhere you go. But you can verbally prepare your child. You can tell him exactly what's going to happen and how you expect him to behave. It's super awesome if you can throw in an easy, immediate task for him to do. This will helps him stay focused.

I was working with Kim, who had three-year-old Alyssa and her six-month-old sister. They had a hot spot in the day of coming home from picking up Alyssa at half-day preschool. It defined chaos. Alyssa was tired and always needed to use the potty but would get distracted, often not even entering the house but running to play in the yard and having accidents. The timing of getting home meant the baby needed to nurse, but Alyssa needed lunch ASAP in order to get down for a nap in time. Everything would fall apart and no one would get what they needed. Kim just felt like she was drowning at that point of the day, and it often ruined the rest of the day. She'd get super short with Alyssa, the baby would be crying, naps would be delayed.

We strategized how to prepare for that huge transition. Kim started preparing a little platter of food for Alyssa before she went to pick her up: a little protein, cut-up fruit and veggies, a little cheese and crackers. This was ready to go in the fridge so she needed no lunch prep (and kids *love* little plates full of little bits of varied food). She started putting the potty chair right by the garage, so when they drove in, it was right there for Alyssa to use.

Then we worked on how to use verbal preparation with

269

Alyssa. The biggest thing to remember is that you must give clear, short directives. Don't overwhelm your child with a huge number of things to do. Don't give any information she doesn't need. For example, Alyssa is three. Kim doesn't have to tell Alyssa that she needs to nurse the baby. Alyssa, being three, doesn't care. This doesn't affect *her* in any way, so it's better to not say anything. We throw too many words at our little ones and expect them to be able to sort out what's important and what's not. Keep the verbal list to what you need from your child.

As they neared home, Kim would tell Alyssa, "When I stop the car at home, you can unbuckle and use the potty. I put it right near the car for you so it will be easy. You will have a big pee. Then take the purple bag and please bring it to the kitchen table. Can you tell me what you will do when I stop the car?"

This phrasing sounds kind of awkward, I know, but there's a specific thing happening. Using the fewest words possible, Kim has prepared Alyssa for the two biggest things that would otherwise start a down spiral for this time of day: the potty and getting in the house. By giving super clear directives (take the purple bag and put it on the kitchen table), we distract the toddler mind.

If you were to say, "help get everything in the house," that would be too much and too unclear. In general, across the board with this age, you need to make your instructions short and specific. "Set the table" is too big. "Can you put a fork next to every plate?" is very doable.

Once Alyssa was in the house, Kim had the plate of food ready. She could nurse the baby while Alyssa ate. But notice something else about the verbal preparation. "You will have a big pee." Not just "go potty" but very specific instructions. Alyssa was incredibly more agreeable to the tasks because they were simple and well-defined—in short, doable for a three-year-old.

If you're not in the practice of breaking things down like this, it can be a lot to think about at first. It is indeed a practice, so be gentle with yourself. You'll soon be in the habit of thinking this way, in short, simple directives that break down the minutiae of a task. Above all, remember that your little one is just learning to process, organize, and prioritize. This is not always your child being difficult. It also reminds us that toddler time is very slow. They need a lot of time and preparation, particularly during transitions. Processing information at this age takes a long time.

While it may feel wonky and time-consuming when you start to do this, just think of how time- and energy-consuming the meltdowns are.

It really can even be as simple as "We will go to the library. We will read one book. Then we will go potty. You will pee in the toilet. You will not be angry. You will not throw a fit. You will wash your hands. And then we will read two more books. And then we will take our books home and leave the library quietly." I've actually had clients say those exact words, "You will not have a fit," and it works! Now remember, this is an overall preparation for your child. In the moment you will use shorter directives. This may seem like a lot of words to give your little one at once (given all I've said about talking too much), but they are very short directives and we're preparing the child, not giving them a task at hand right now.

To this day, my clients say this is by far the best tool for dealing with toddlers. It's been field-tested, people. With many. Like everything else, it's a practice. Not every single transition is going to go well.

As I hope you know by now, we can't always control and

mitigate behavior. Our little ones have moods and knee-jerk reactions like all humans do. But this sort of verbal preparation, once it becomes part of your routine, can rock your world. It can feel very awkward and strange at first, so again, it takes practice, but soon you'll be helping your child through these wonky transitions with ease.

Use timers

I find timers to be extremely useful both for children and for us. Because just about all of us have a smartphone, it's not challenging to use a timer. One of the best areas in life to use one is the warning times when you have to prompt and prepare your child to leave a place or activity. Too often we say "five minutes," which means anything from two minutes to a half hour, if we get talking with another grown-up. Though toddlers don't have a sense of time yet, they are fully aware that you have prepped them to leave but now you're not leaving. This is adding another mini transition to the leaving time. If you've warned them plenty and they've processed all the prompts, they don't have the grace and skill to say, "Oh, okay. I can see you're talking, Mom, so I'll just occupy myself for a few more minutes." That would be awesome if they could, but think toddler here for a minute.

It took them a while to process leaving. They are *now ready to go.* Asking them to play a little longer while you chat is *an entirely different thing.* They can't turn on a dime yet. They're not flexible in their thinking. And then *you will ask them to leave again.* Do you see what I mean? We've mucked up the transition they were prepared for.

A timer is a great reminder not just for them but for us to haul ass out of there. It has an additional bonus of getting their bodies and brains in a rhythm of time. If you are consistent with five minutes actually being five minutes, your child's body will naturally start to lock into that zone. Which in the long run will remove some of the struggles.

Welcome transitional objects

I'd like to add a bit about transitional objects, since we are in fact talking about making transitions easy. You probably are familiar with this concept even if you didn't know the clinical term for it. These are objects children take with them to ease transitions. A blankie, a stuffed animal, a rock—it can be anything. It can be the object that your little can't seem to live without or it can be just any little something. It may seem like your kid can't walk out the door without taking something from home.

And that's just it. *They are taking a piece of home with them.* To make the transition easier for themselves. It's almost a natural thing that happens. You may not have even noticed until I pointed it out, and now you're like *Oh. Yeah. My little one always needs to grab something!*

Transitional objects are the *best*. It's totally fine for your child to carry a transitional object with her. It's also okay to have some rules about when Beary has to stay in the car and wait. These objects are a bridge for your child. Taking a piece of home with her makes her more comfortable with leaving.

They are also a phenomenal tool when your child goes to day care or preschool. Even if your little one has been in day care for most of his life, he can still all of a sudden, out of the blue get separation anxiety. And some kids aren't in any day care/group setting until it's time for preschool. And still other kids won't be in that setting until kindergarten. Most day care/

school settings won't allow a blankie or bear in the room (some allow them for nap times). In these instances, I've found an amazing way to help your child transition. You can get a small object and infuse it with mom or dad love.

This object can be a small rock, crystal, jewel, if they have pockets, or can even be a bracelet or something else they wear. I personally used a small rose-quartz heart-shaped stone for Pascal. He was happy enough to have it in his lunch box, but your child may want something he can keep close. You "fill" it with your love and give it to your child in the morning when he goes to school. Then he gives it back to you when he gets home and you fill it again. You can fill it any way you choose. Some parents put it under their pillow; some hold it and purposefully show the child they are filling it. It doesn't much matter how you fill it; think toddler here and you'll be fine.

Here's the really great bonus part of this. This transitional object is also a fantastic way to gauge your little one's day. It doubles as a transitional object when you get back home. You can make a small practice of taking back the object to fill it. Your child might say something like "It's really, really empty today." This gives you *vital* information as to how her day went. Without asking the ubiquitous and generally useless question "How was your day?" you can instantly tell that she needs some snuggles and love. Alternately, your child may exclaim, "It's still full!" and again, you've gotten some good information.

This is probably one of my tools that is used the most. It's really, really effective for helping with those wonky transitions.

The Big Takeaway

Slow down, way down. Toddler time is very slow. If transitions are crazy, think slower. The more you can prepare your child with short, doable directives, the more you can start to iron out daily transitions. Breaking down the minutiae of a task can feel awkward and time-consuming at first, but it's far better to use your time helping your child be successful rather than dealing with a cranky and uncooperative toddler.

CHAPTER 19

FOOD AND BEHAVIOR

No, this chapter is not about what you should or shouldn't be feeding your child. I trust that you are making the best decisions for your family in regard to food. I specifically want to talk about two areas concerning food that I regularly see in my practice. The first is how to deal with food allergies and sensitivities that affect behavior. And the second is how to have mealtimes that don't suck the life out of you.

Allergies and sensitivities

I would be horribly remiss in talking about toddler behavior without mentioning rising food sensitivities and allergies, and the importance of gut health. There are many theories as to why there is such an uptick in food sensitivities, and they alone would fill an entire book. I would say I call a food allergy in one in three of my clients. And by that I mean I have them go to a doctor to see if one is present. I am not nor do I claim to be an expert in food allergies. What I am expert at is looking for answers when I see behavior that is way out of the normal range.

277

One of the big things I look for is super frequent tantrums that go from zero to sixty in three seconds, over very minor things. Remember: tantrums are developmentally appropriate in the two- to three-year-old range. By four, tantrums should start easing off as your child gets better language and communication skills. Kids this age become more physically skilled, so small tasks don't frustrate them. And they also are continually developing self-control. Tantrums are huge feelings or manipulations that your little one doesn't yet have the skills to articulate or negotiate with words. It's like system collision and will often take even your child by surprise.

Developmentally speaking, a few tantrums a month are normal. While there's a range of normal and abnormal behaviors during a tantrum, the frequency of tantrums is the biggest indicator that something is off. If your child is tantrumming several times a day or even many times throughout the week, that is of concern.

In my practice I find much confusion; many parents have, of course, heard that tantrums are normal. So they believe that regardless of how often it's happening, it's all within normal range. This is not the case. In regard to abnormal tantrums, there can be an underlying psychological problem. Of course, first we look at big changes or upsets in the child's life. Divorce or separation, a new school, a big move, a new baby—any big stressors can trigger abnormal tantrums. But largely speaking, you'll know the cause and the tantrums are the sudden-onset variety. Your average-behaved toddler starts epic tantrums the minute the new baby enters your world. Those dots aren't hard to connect.

The other reason for abnormal tantrums can be a gut/gastrointestinal problem linked to a food intolerance. I like to jump into food first before a potential behavioral diagnosis because in my experience, it's usually the cause and it's a much easier fix.

Most parents *hate* investigating allergies and sensitivities. Going down this rabbit hole usually means a dietary overhaul and that sucks. However, when my clients dive into these changes, the improvement is near miraculous in most cases.

Food allergies and sensitivities have gotten a bad rap because some people can be a total pain in the ass about them. It's pretty commonplace now for gluten or nut allergies to be recognized. And I'm going to go off on a tangent here because I'm pretty tired of people trying to take down the gluten-free thing. You can absolutely be sensitive to gluten/wheat and not have celiac. Celiac means you are *completely intolerant* of the gluten protein. It will make you sick and/or land you in the hospital. A relatively small percentage of people have celiac. There's a whole slew of us who are *sensitive* to the protein to a greater or lesser degree. I say *us* because I am one of them. When I have gluten, my stomach bloats to the size of a five-month pregnancy. I get diarrhea and a feeling like a lead ball is hanging out by my anus. I get dark circles under my eyes and my arthritis pain kicks in to the point of my not being able to hold a pen in my hand. And it makes me cranky AF. For real. And I'm a grown-up who has a good handle on my moods and emotional regulation.

Food allergies and sensitivities not only wreak havoc with the reactions you can see—i.e., eczema, rashes, respiratory issues, itchy eyes, swollen joints, etc.—they can wreak havoc on your whole digestive track. This is hard on anyone, but imagine being a little one, feeling that yucky but having no words for it.

This can result in crazy behavior and the other bane of your toddler-life existence: picky eating. I first dove into gut and GI issues in my potty training work. Regularly loose, frequent stools often indicate a food allergy or sensitivity. When we would tweak the child's diet, a miraculous thing happened: behavior changed in a way neither I nor the parents I was working with could have imagined. Time and time again, I kept hearing, "It's like I have a different kid!"

The major offenders for food allergies and sensitivities are gluten/wheat, soy, eggs, shellfish, citrus fruits, tree nuts, dairy, and chocolate. Food dyes can also be the culprit behind whack-adoodle behavior.

The biggest problem is that you can test negative for a "true allergy" and still be sensitive to a food. Not all food intolerances show up as anaphylactic shock or rashes or anything externally obvious. They can cause internal distress that can make your child crazy.

Karen first contacted me for potty training help. Her little one, Liam, was constantly having blow-out poop accidents. As we started working, I learned he was not only pooping up to four times a day, he was also having four or five major meltdowns a day that seemed to come out of the blue. We discussed food sensitivities, and Karen took him for allergy testing. He appeared to have no food allergies. Karen was relentless, though, and started a basic elimination diet. This consisted of a pretty simple diet of plain proteins and vegetables. Within days, Liam's poop became normal—once or twice a day, well-formed—and he wasn't having accidents. But much to both of our surprise, his meltdowns stopped. He was still a normal three-year-old, mind you, but the epic emotional breakdowns stopped. As Karen added in more varied foods, she quickly hit the issue—chocolate and citrus. Liam didn't eat a ton of chocolate, but even the smallest taste and boom! Poop everywhere. He did love oranges, but the first day she added in an orange, same thing. Poop disaster and an emotional puddle.

He didn't test as allergic to these foods. They seem like pretty random innocuous foods. Karen never did get answers as to why those foods or what exactly was happening internally for Liam. But all in all, she was pretty thrilled that she'd trusted her instinct that both his pooping and behavior were food-related.

I can't overstate this. Food intolerances can wreak all kinds of havoc on your child's internal and external state. Identifying the problem and fixing it can change previously picky eaters into chowhounds. It can change what looks like crappy toddler behavior. It can change crazy power struggles into charming days. It can change everything for you.

In reality, what are you looking for?

If there are no big external reactions (such as a rash), what are some hints that diet could be the underlying issue in your child's behavior?

- Your gut instinct. Something, anything feels off to you. You look around at other kids and you think something along the lines of *I wish it were that easy.*
- Zero-to-sixty behavior. Meltdowns that slam you out of the blue. These will be long and drawn-out. They will be all the time. You feel like you're drowning in battles with your child on a daily basis.
- Unexplainable meltdowns or tantrums. Tantrums should have a semi-apparent source—high frustration, trying to control other humans who won't comply, wanting something you won't give, etc. If your child

falls apart because you say good morning or blink, this might indicate inner discomfort. If your child regularly melts down over nothing, it's worth digging deeper.

- Constant tantrums. Four to six tantrums a month are developmentally appropriate. If your little one is having massive tantrums daily, you definitely want to experiment with diet. Of course, other things can be at play as well. Make sure your child is getting adequate sleep and plenty of Big Play. Have there been big changes in your child's life?
- Big energy swings, particularly patterned around eating times. Does your child eat and then take a big downward or upward swing? Does your toddler often experience episodes of lethargy? Or the flip side? Huge spikes where they spiral up and up and look a little kooky?
- Struggles with pooping. Does your child poop more than three times a day? Have frequent accidents? Have loose stools with visible food chunks?

Looking at diet can feel overwhelming. In all my work we start by looking for patterns. Start noticing if there's any regularity to the crazy behavior—times of day or after a meal or snack. You may need to keep a chart to track behavior, because I know the whole day can often feel out of control. A chart will give you clues as to whether or not diet might be playing into behavior.

Experimenting with diet is one of the few things you can do on your own that have no ramifications except inconvenience. I am in no way suggesting that dietary changes are a cure-all. I'm in no way suggesting that dietary changes should be the only thing you look into if you suspect something is off with your

FOOD AND BEHAVIOR

child's behavior. My experience with other families is largely anecdotal, with recreational research I've done on my own as I've worked with families. With all that said, I have seen small miracles happen in families when they find the right nutritional tweaks and solutions. I know people have strong feelings about food and eating and often are very resistant to changing their eating habits. Remember, I opened this section with the words "I would be remiss" if I didn't include this information.

Dinners that don't suck the life out of you

Does dinnertime stress you out? Does your little one hem and haw and make dinner less than a stellar experience? Yes, eating meals with our children is a huge part of family life. However, thanks to hectic schedules, most families are eating dinner way too late for toddlers. This not only makes for an unpleasant mealtime, it also pushes bedtime back. I talked about this problem in chapter 14. It definitely bears revisiting.

I suggest a radical and life-altering solution: Feed the children earlier. Like way earlier, four or five o'clock earlier. Hear me out. When we think about meals with our kids, we have a few things in play—connection, healthy food choices, and table manners.

We also know they are usually starving around four and then seemingly not hungry at dinnertime. If your child is ravenous at four, feed her more than a snack; feed her dinner. It doesn't have to be a glamorous meal, just real food. Then, come dinnertime, she can have her *snack* with you at the table. Because she's already eaten her nutritious meal earlier, you can enjoy the connection with your child, instead of endless pushing for "just one more bite, please."

This fix can look a million different ways according to your family and your schedule. If both parents work outside the home, it may mean packing a "second lunch" for your child at preschool afternoon snack time. If one parent stays home, that parent can feed the child earlier. When the other parent gets home, that parent can have quality connection time with the child or head right into bedtime routine. It may mean serving your little one heated leftovers or a simple platter with veggies, fruit, protein. Or maybe even just a sandwich.

The big motive for family meals is end-of-the-day connection with our kids. But if your meals are miserable, is that the connection you're seeking? It's far better to feed them earlier and make the evenings about play, stories, and settling down. Weekend meals can be a huge connection time. If your mornings are scrunched for time, breakfast can be the family meal.

We are hammered with the idea that family meals are vitally important. And I agree. They become particularly important as our kids get older and pull away from us, with activities and friends. But at the preschooler age, taking care of the actual hunger much earlier and then freeing up the evening for good connection can be more important. And if you're struggling to achieve an earlier bedtime, this is most definitely your answer. There's plenty of time in your child's life for the lovely dinners you envision. For this period of time, it's much better to work with what your child needs.

The Big Takeaway

Food can absolutely affect behavior both for good and for bad. Trust your intuition. If something feels off, the tantrums seem too explosive or too frequent, try investigating food both in timing and for sensitivities. This is too huge a topic to cover here, but if you suspect it may be relevant to your family, even the most cursory search on how gut health affects behavior can point you to some answers.

MY FINAL WORDS:
YOU GOT THIS

My parting words for you. I think this part is supposed to sound extraordinarily wise. I don't know if I can pull that off. With all my own parenting and my professional expertise, I want you to know I'm still down there in the trenches with you. I never want to seem like this lofty expert up on her high horse. I always say and will continue to say: You are the expert on your child. Never lose sight of that. I have worked with hundreds of families, which gives me a wider scope of vision, but I don't know your unique individual toddler. You know your child best.

My aim is always to give you tips, tricks, and tools to ease the way—not to impose laws, edicts, or judgments. We all do our best. I believe that with all my heart.

In my own parenting, I have big goals and grand ideas for parenting that never fully pan out. I lose my shit too. But that doesn't mean we stop striving for better.

These are the years it can feel like you're drowning. Or maybe just barely keeping your head above water. I know parents love behavior Band-Aids at this age. Help me fix this right now!

Band-Aids are sometimes necessary, for sure, but my goal in this book is to give you a myriad of tools for working from the inside out. For building a really strong foundation, not just for now but for the future as well. Not one of these tools is an unfailing immediate fix. But then again, parenting is a long game, even when the end of day seems never to come.

Parenting is a practice. Daily, we have a chance to hone our skills, to get better. It evolves. As new as your little one is to the world, you're *that* new as a parent. It gets better, I promise.

Like playing an instrument, doing yoga, meditating, working out, learning any new skill, parenting takes practice and patience. You don't come out of the gates a pro. There are repetitive drills that suck but lay the routine and groundwork. There are days where you're, like, *Damn. I'm good!* And there are days you cry because *Really? How can I suck so bad at this?*

Listen to me. You don't have to be perfect. For real.

The biggest thing you need to do is love and honor that child in front you. At the end of the day, that's what really matters.

If I had to leave you with a cheat sheet to keep in your pocket or on your fridge, it would be this:

Remember how young and new your child is to everything! Kids don't know as much as we may think. That doesn't mean they're stupid, though. Respect your little one as you would any other human. That respect will come back to you in a beautiful way.

All behavior is communication. Even jerk behavior. Look for the why, try to translate. Keep connection with your child, and ease up on being the constant mistake monitor.

Playing and exploring are essential, and 100 percent better than formal academics; learning takes precedence over education at this age.

Be open to changing course. If what you're doing isn't working, try something else. It's okay to change your ideas and philosophy. Raising a human is a moving target. Ditch anything that's not working for you—including judgy friends, crazy sched-ules, and anything that makes you feel less than your best self.

And finally, I want to give you a small piece of advice that a wise mama gave me years ago: "Don't worry, you won't fuck this up. You can't. I promise." Love and stay connected and you really, seriously won't fuck this up. So take that off your plate right now.

And seriously. Sleep more.

Rock on, you badass mamas and papas.

YOU GOT THIS.

ACKNOWLEDGMENTS

No one does it alone. It takes a village. In my case, many villages.

My personal village: Thank you for feeding my kid, talking me down, and all the convos about parenting our kids; my mom, my auntie Sue, Amanda, Cheryl, Jen, Melissa, Caitlyn. And especially Eva . . . for the endless cappuccino.

My professional village: Thank you to my ah-mazing agent, Allison Hunter, for translating my crazy into my nice words. Every time. Thanks for all you've done for me. My editors: Cara Bedick, for seeing the original vision and all the shaping, and Lauren Spiegel, for crossing the finish line with me. And, OMG, Rebecca Strobel! Gurl . . . you need anything, you call me. I got your back like you had mine.

Thank you, gorgeous Sara Yamich, for my FB ads, the dance, and being an unflinching cheerleader. The fabulous Tamika Auwai, for seeing the huge vision and helping me get there. And, Lord, thank you so much for Amy Jones, my tireless assistant, who fielded all outside communication for me while I wrote and wrote.

My online village: Thank you Kelly the Most Excellent, Meghan #yaledit, Hannah—the Best Worst Mom Ever, Jenny the Fancy, and Holly Most Holly for keeping me laughing. And just because: Kim, Denise, Colleen, Juana, Curly Karen,

ACKNOWLEDGMENTS

Maryanne, Cynthia, Rhiannon, Carli, Carly, Jane, Jennifer, Anglea, and Meggan.

My fitness village: the OCR racing team and coaches of Laid-back Fitness for literally keep me sane and in fighting shape.

I hope I'm not forgetting anyone. If we've ever crossed paths, had a moment, or you've made me laugh, *thank you.*

ABOUT THE AUTHOR

Jamie Glowacki is the author of the popular *Oh Crap! Potty Training*. Her two former careers as circus performer and social worker make her uniquely qualified to deal with toddlers. She lives in Providence, Rhode Island, with her crazy cool kid, Pascal. For all things parenting and potty training, visit www.jamieglowacki.com.

Read more from
Jamie Glowacki

Pick up or download your copy today!

GALLERY BOOKS
An Imprint of Simon & Schuster
A CBS COMPANY